The Crisis in Religious Vocations:

An Inside View

Edited by

Laurie Felknor

New York ◆ *Paulist Press* ◆ *Mahwah*

The publisher gratefully acknowledges use of material condensed from the chapter "Vanishing Church Professionals," from the book *The Sociologist Looks at Religion* © 1988 by Joseph H. Fichter, S.J. Reprinted by permission of Michael Glazier, Inc.

BX 2380
C73
1989

Library of Congress Cataloging-in-Publication Data

The Crisis in religious vocations : an inside view / edited by Laurie
   Felknor.
       p.   cm.
   Includes bibliographies.
   ISBN 0-8091-3073-4 : $8.95 (est.)
   1. Monastic and religious life.   2. Vocation, Ecclesiastical.
   I. Felknor, Laurie.
   BX2380.C73   1989
   255′.00973′09048—dc20   89-8727
                                                         CIP

Published by Paulist Press
997 Macarthur Boulevard
Mahwah, NJ 07430

Printed and bound in the
United States of America

ACKNOWLEDGEMENT

The publishers acknowledge their indebtedness to Sister Bette Moslander CSJ, of the Sisters of St. Joseph of Concordia, Kansas. Sister Moslander was a member of the Advisory Committee to the Pontifical Commission appointed by Pope John Paul II in 1983 to study the decline in the number of religious vocations among men and women in the United States. It was she who coordinated and facilitated this Study. We are grateful to Sister Moslander as well for sending to us the thirty-four reflective essays written by men and women religious for the Study, from which we have chosen sixteen to include in this volume.

CONTENTS

Part One
The Vocation Crisis: An Introduction

v

CONTENTS

Part Two
Factors of Change, Past and Present

Part Three
Perspectives on the Decline of Vocations

CONTENTS

Editor's Note

The essays presented here have been selected and condensed from papers prepared for a summary that ultimately contributed to a report to the Holy Father by the Pontifical Commission on Religious Life. All the priests and religious who were asked to write papers were invited to examine data which included a study prepared for the Center for Applied Research in the Apostolate (CARA) by Joseph J. Shields, Ph.D. and Mary Jeanne Verdieck, Ph.D. entitled *Religious Life in the United States: The Experience of Men's Communities*, and a book by Marie Augusta Neal, SND de Namur entitled *Catholic Sisters in Transition: From the 1960s to the 1980s* (Michael Glazier). Then all were asked to respond to the same two questions: Why did religious leave their congregations? Why are young people not entering in greater numbers?

We have attempted to present, from among the papers, a variety of reflections on these two questions, drawn from different disciplines and perspectives.

Introduction

In June of 1983, the Holy Father created a Pontifical Commission on Religious Life comprised of Archbishop Thomas C. Kelly, O.P., Bishop Raymond Lessard and myself. We were given two tasks. First, we were asked to assist the diocesan bishops of the United States in offering "special pastoral service" to the religious men and women in their local churches. In addition, we were to pursue a study of the reasons for the decline in vocations to religious life and why young people were not entering in greater numbers.

In our effort to fulfill the second task, we assembled the factual, sociological data available in regard to the two questions. This data, then, was given to a group of nearly forty experts in various fields—theology, canon law, scripture, psychology and psychiatry, history, church history, philosophy, sociology and others. All these experts were priests or religious with one or two exceptions. They were asked to review the data and on the basis of their expertise and their own experience to develop a paper in light of the main question proposed: Why the decline in religious vocations? Why do not more young people enter religious life?

The papers were circulated among the group of experts and subsequently they were convened in a meeting in San Francisco to share their views for the benefit of the Pontifical Commission. Following the San Francisco meeting, a summary of the papers and of the discussion which took place during that meeting was prepared. This summary was sent to a representative group of bishops, religious, priests and lay people in some fifteen dioceses in the United States for their reaction. In addition, the Pontifical Commission also consulted with the Committee of Religious with which it worked closely in the fulfillment of its mandate.

INTRODUCTION

Having listened to all these various voices, the Pontifical Commission formed its own judgment and developed a report for the Holy Father responding to the questions mentioned above.

Some of the papers which went into this effort are now published here. They are not papers of the Pontifical Commission. They do not necessarily represent or reflect the views of the Pontifical Commission. But they were employed by the Pontifical Commission in an effort to see the problem from various points of view and in an effort to reach an informed judgment. Once again, I express gratitude to those who assisted us so generously.

Most Reverend John R. Quinn
Archbishop of San Francisco

Part One

The Vocation Crisis: An Introduction

Fewer Vocations: Crisis or Challenge?

Sarah Marie Sherman, R.S.M.

The period of the 1960s was one of intense and rapid ferment. Although I leave to the historians and sociologists the analysis of the impact of change in the mid-century, two events seem to stand out in most discussions of the climate of U.S. Catholicism in the 1960s: the election of John F. Kennedy, a Catholic, to the U.S. presidency, and the convening of the Second Vatican Council. Kennedy's election signaled the beginning of a new era—the fading of a distinctive Catholic subculture and the assimilation of Catholicism into the American middle class.

The Second Vatican Council, in its efforts to renew the church and call it to adapt to the monumental changes in cultures, societies and religious awareness, initiated reforms in veritably every aspect of church life, ranging from ecumenism, liturgy and communications to even the church's own understanding of itself as the people of God. Few, if any, had an intuition of how far-reaching the impact of renewal would be, and two of the groups most profoundly affected were the women and men religious.

Religious Prior to Vatican II

If Catholics prior to the 1960s were a subculture within U.S. society, then the religious were a subculture within a subculture. The promulgation of the Code of Canon Law in 1917, while effectively eliminating or limiting a number of abuses through strict codification and regulation, also served

5

to institutionalize and harness the spirit and practice of women and men religious. Regulations, prescriptions and horaria eventually became ends in themselves. The spirit of rugged individualism was subsumed by the necessity of conformity for unity's sake. Stability was evident, not only in the church, but in religious life as well. The men and women religious were the respectable, dependable and highly efficient apostolic adjunct to a strong and rigid hierarchy. The church was organized into a neat hierarchy, and everyone knew his or her place within the order. The entire faith system was buttressed by an elaborate and well-ordered set of symbols and rituals. Such organization imparted a sense of security and justification to many if not all Catholics. A step into religious life connoted status and security for a person (although other more generous motives were most often also present), and he or she was moving one rung higher from the bottom of the Catholic organizational system. Religious also had a long tradition and high reputation for charitable works. Popularity and ranks grew yearly. The price to be paid for this success was the continued agreement to live a semi-cloistered life, easily regulated from within and without, and which, in many regards, was segregated from the "secular" realities which threatened to weaken it.

The subculture of religious life was well established. Numbers peaked in seminaries and novitiates. Many religious communities embarked upon ambitious building projects in the early 1960s to house and maintain the eager young candidates. Most were never able to use these buildings for the purpose for which they were intended. What happened?

Religious and Vatican II

In one sense, the changes initiated by Vatican II were only the tip of the iceberg. Even if the council had not taken place, it seemed that religious life had long passed the dynamic equilibrium for great stability and size at the same time. For too long it had been insulated from many of the dizzying aspects of societal change. The first hole in the dike was probably initiated already in the 1950s with the Sister Formation Movement which challenged and enabled many women religious to become professionally prepared, often beyond their peers in church ministry. The most identifiable catalyst for this movement was obviously the council's Decree on the Renewal of Religious Life, *Perfectae Caritatis*. In this wise and monumental document, religious were mandated to return to the sources of the whole of Christian life and to the primitive spirit and charism of their foundresses and founders. Adaptation to the changed conditions of our time was a directive, not a suggestion.[1]

The response on the part of the religious, women even more so than men, was enthusiastic. The women moved more quickly in general, for possibly two reasons: their preparation for new ideas and values through the higher education thrust in the Sister Formation Movement, and their mostly unconscious intuition at that time, because of the position of women in society in general and the church in particular, that they had more issues to process. What followed is history, familiar enough to most of us: special chapters, new directives, periods of experimentation. The mood and spirit was euphoric, at least for several years, until the weight of such rapid change, for all the reasons cited earlier, made itself felt. The tensions and difficulties of the profound societal and ecclesial upheaval in the 1960s was telescoped into religious life.

The first and most dramatic effects of the change were experienced: open disputes became more common, polarization in communities appeared, increasing numbers of persons left religious life, the number of candidates approaching religious life was sharply declining. In fact, these signs seemed almost correlated to the rapidity with which particular groups

7

entered into the process of renewal. Those who held back, as it were, experienced these traumas to a much lesser degree, at least in the beginning. These observable differences in communities along the continuum of change and adaptation provided one of the most frustrating obstacles to the unity and support needed among different religious communities and between religious and the laity. Because the initial signs of renewal represented for many a departure from what had come to symbolize orthodoxy and stability in the church, the changes themselves were often judged to be destructive and the products of discontented persons. "If these things are happening, then we (you) must be doing something wrong." Those who held back from renewal and adaptation experienced instead the affirmation and approval of those who were threatened and disoriented by the societal and ecclesial ferment. The religious who were not changing along with everything else became for many a sign, a retreat into anxious security.

A Model of Development

Dr. Bernard Boelen, drawing insight from the late Cardinal Suhard, concludes that the unrest that we have been experiencing in the church and religious life is not a sickness, nor a self-destruction of the church, but a *crisis of growth*. "It is the decisive period of an impetuous adolescence."

Boelen explains that the essence of adolescence is the painful but wonderful emergence of the person (spirit) out of the functional level of existence (puberty). In human development, the beginning adolescent lives in a world characterized by logical thinking and organizing action, its structures and systems, and the "sameness" of the universal applicability of its laws and concepts. The children leaving childhood are "spectators" of reality. They love to argue and debate, but the debate is not yet the authentic dialogue in which participants are striving together for truth. Instead it is a competitive contest.

Early puberty is filled with ritualism, a ritualism which is objectified ritual, ritual without celebration, reduced to magic and taken out of context. The society of puberty consists in "fair play," the strict conformity to the unwritten rules and regulations of the gang. Not the spirit but the letter of the law reigns.

The parallel with the pre-conciliar church, hopefully, is obvious. Doing the correct thing was given priority over being the whole person. Holiness was defined in terms of a legalistic and stifling conformity, Boelen asserts, to a body of doctrine, a static set of rules or the status quo of the establishment. Catholics experienced themselves as individuals of the same "species"—Roman Catholic. They mistook unity for uniformity or sameness, and wanted the same dress ("habits"), the same language, the same ritualism, and even the same sex!

At the other end of the process, maturity begins to emerge when the adolescent experiences primordial wonder, the all-encompassing mystery of the gift of the Spirit; he or she discovers himself or herself and others as *person*. Maturity is not the end of growing, but the beginning of the full-grown way of growing. The adolescent discovers his or her own "uniqueness" and "response-ability." "Truth" is no longer conformity to a thing but a creative self-revelation of the Spirit. "Good" is no longer doing the correct thing, but being the integral person. Faithfulness is no longer a mechanical, unchanging adherence to the status quo, but the "creative fidelity" of personal involvement.[2]

Likewise, for the church and religious life, the above insights and attitudes are rapidly transforming our structures, our ways of organizing ourselves, our ministry, our relationships with one another. Less and less is the person subordi-

9

nated to the structure, the institution, the rigid regulation. Highly significant is the simple realization that since Vatican II we no longer define the church in terms of an institution, but in terms of the people of God. In our deepening awareness of the primacy of person, we are in the process of turning around our entire understanding of what vocation really entails. Each person, called individually by a loving God through creation and baptism, is endowed with unique rights and responsibilities within the communion of God's people. No longer do we understand the primary invitation as one of obedience to laws and regulations, but instead to be one of loving and self-sacrificing service to one another.

There is an important ramification to all of this: the process of maturation, in which we now find ourselves as Christians and religious, does not happen easily, quickly, or without great difficulty. On the way out of adolescence, Boelen says, we pass through a "dark night" or a period of anxiety and meaninglessness. In letting go of the "old ways"of childhood, we pass through a hiatus, a tunnel, a desert on our way to the "new ways" of adulthood. For adolescents, that means boredom, restlessness and confusion. They don't like themselves because they are not yet at home and familiar with the selves they are becoming. Where once they were sure of themselves as children and their value system was functional and served them well, they no longer know what their values are. Insecurity can take over and the confused adolescent can become either rebellious or withdrawn—and can believe that nobody really likes or cares about her or him. The temptation is to "go back" to values and behaviors that were secure. Regression sometimes emerges for a while. If it becomes chronic, the situation is problematic. However, the great majority of young persons hang in there, because they do recognize some signs of life and growth within themselves. Through fidelity to the process and oneself, the adolescent does slowly begin to integrate the various aspects of his or her life into a meaningful and fulfilling whole.

If we can accept this model of development as describing our journey as a people within the church and in religious life through the last twenty years, then many of our experiences can take on new meaning. As we said earlier, because the religious had been, as it were, a highly regulated and institutionalized subculture within a subculture, their embrace of the renewal called for in the church was more rapid, enthusiastic and radical than for other groups within the church. Within several years they were beginning to feel the full weight of the results of their efforts toward renewal. The religious had begun first, and most fully, a profound *identity shift*. Their movement from a level of a more impersonal, structured, legalistic way of being to a more personal, mature and holistic embodiment of life and ministry moved them into the desert of identity crisis. The old ways no longer satisfied, nor did they believe that the God of their lives and experience was calling them back to the past. They had begun a journey of renewal in response to the mandate of their church, and with definite conviction, and sometimes little understanding, they knew they had to be faithful to that journey. Continuing on the journey, there have often been temptations to turn back; the voices of security are deafening from without and within.

Relationship to Vocations

Within this experience of identity crisis, a necessary aspect of the movement of growth of an individual or a group of people, we find some of the apparent reasons for the present numerical decline in the number of persons choosing to enter religious life.

In examining the research around this issue, one factor emerges as principal when we describe the major reason why persons are not considering vowed/ordained ministry in the church today: *lack of encouragement* from significant others. Lack of encouragement relates to our discussion of identity shift among religious in at least two important ways:

(a) In moving through the "desert" or transitional phase of the growth process, the experience is one of withdrawal and confusion—about oneself, about one's community, about the church. Finding themselves in a hiatus or experiential void, having left behind some of the values and practices that gave stability and purpose to their life before, many religious were thrust into periods of skepticism about themselves, their vocations, their communities and the wisdom of their choices at this time. Few or none had been adequately prepared for the depth of discernment that would be required of them. This phenomenon created crises of confidence both within and outside the religious communities. ("If people are leaving, there must be something wrong.")

(b) In addition, the religious, being ahead of the laity in renewal (because at that time the laity were dependent upon the clergy and religious to exert any leadership—a situation which apparently is beginning to reverse itself), were becoming less credible to the laity. Manner of dress was changing for many religious. Modes of religious education were rapidly undergoing modification. New understandings of ministry and ministerial needs were shifting some religious away from established works into new areas, and in particular away from education and service to the upper and middle classes. In reality, the overall shifts were minor, but to those affected most directly they appeared much greater. Some even believed that the religious were intentionally "abandoning" them.

These experiences were leading many of the laity to be confused about religious who were actively taking part in the renewal. They withdrew their moral and financial support from them and shifted their affirmation to those groups who

were resistant to renewal and who thus provided greater identification with the secure church of the past. Obviously, one of
the last things that laypeople would do would be to encourage
their sons or daughters or students to become a religious
priest, brother or sister.

Those religious who remained in religious life frequently
experienced the skepticism of those earlier years. Sometimes I
heard statements like: "I don't know what my community
values anymore." "I would never encourage someone to enter
our community today!"

Although religious and parents still appear to be affected
by the confusion, we observe indications that the young persons themselves are not so adversely affected by these changes.
First, as indicated by their age (the median age for those
entering today hovers around twenty-seven or twenty-eight),
most have little experience of the trauma of the radical shifts of
renewal in their own lives. They are a generation growing up
in the midst of value shifts and change of every sort. They are
also a generation coming of age in a church which is growing
slowly into personalism and a deepening spiritual maturity.
Although still fewer in number, they are a group who can
identify, not with the religious communities of the stable pre-
Vatican days, but with the religious communities as they are
maturing, through suffering and being misunderstood. Current research has shown that those women who choose to enter
today find the community's support for gospel values and their
stance on social justice to be highly influential in their choice.
Those women who consider religious life *after* high school,
after they are no longer under the direct influence of their
parents and their ambivalence, are more likely to follow
through on the choice. The most recent survey of young Catholics indicates that they are not "turned off" by confusion about
the role of religious and priests today.

These young people are also being helped today by many

communities who have moved in fidelity through much of the shift and are now discerning and setting definite direction for themselves. Shields and Verdieck note that communities which have methodically evaluated their present situation in terms of personnel and resources and who have involved themselves in clarifying the value and uniqueness of their own identity are more successful in attracting vocations. "These are the communities who know where they have come from, are aware of where they are presently and who are proactively determining their own preferred futures."[3]

I believe that what we discover here is a profile of a new candidate for religious life, one who is escaping the identity confusion of the past years, or who is making choices out of an autonomy and/or spiritual perception that sees beyond the questions. It may be that this also partially explains why more and more of those who enter religious life today are thirty years old or older. Perhaps many of these needed the time and additional maturity and experience to "weather the storm," as it were; perhaps they unconsciously perceived the need for more signs of depth and maturity in religious communities and in themselves—and with time they are discovering it.

A Reflection. Upon first examination of the trend away from permanency and celibacy, I am somewhat puzzled. It is obvious that there are few role models for permanency evident in today's society, and that the brokenness of people's lives often brings them to doubt seriously their capacity for permanency in any type of relationship. However, with the poor track record that marriage has these days, I wonder why people aren't flocking to celibate lifestyles and the seeming independence they provide. One apparent reason is the supersaturation of our culture with sexual values and fulfillment "overkill." Subtly, the present generation (and those to come?) are being led to believe that life without sex is a life without anything. Possibly a deeper reason that needs to be explored more closely in relation to vocation decisions is an underlying sense of insecurity in many of today's youth. The cultural influences and changes of which we spoke earlier have taken their toll not only on Catholics, obviously. The brokenness of many people's lives leads them to doubt their capacity for permanency. Is it possible that it also leads them to question deeply their capacity to achieve happiness and wholeness without the close and intense support of one other person? Or is it possible that considerably fewer persons than once believed can grow happily and healthily in vowed celibacy? Perhaps our numbers today are a truer indication of an authentic call to live celibacy.

Rise of Lay Ministry. One of the presently exciting correlaries to the observations above is the unprecedented increase in the number of persons choosing church service in the form of lay ministry. This phenomenon could be a cause, a result, or—most probably—both, as related to the decline in numbers of those choosing vowed life and ministry. In Vatican II's Constitution on the Church, *Lumen Gentium*, the lay vocation was restored to its long-denied position of sharing equally in the call to holiness.[4]

Many, including myself, have asserted that the decline in number of priests and religious was necessary in order for the laity to emerge into their rightful place in the life and ministry of the church. The role accorded to the "religious professionals" as the work force and leadership vanguard of the church was too engrained in us, until we were "forced" to let go and "allow" the laity to join us as partners in church ministry.

Dean Hoge's study of Catholic college students reports that almost seventy percent express an interest in careers as lay ministers. "This means that in the total Catholic population the pool of people currently interested in full-time ministries is about fifty times as large as the pool of people interested in [vowed/ordained] vocations.[5]

How do we interpret this? Do we discourage vocations to lay ministry and leadership so that numbers of persons choosing vowed life might increase once again? Few would recommend such an approach, although it is difficult to observe two positive movements "competing," as it were, with one another. It has been observed that when all vocations, in particular now those of the laity, find their rightful place and support within the church, then all vocations will thrive in proper perspective. We do not rise by stepping on one another. More than ever, the laity are needed to share their charisms, gifts and dedication with all God's people. As they are strengthened and grow, so will the religious vocation—perhaps numerically, perhaps not, we need more time to see—but most assuredly the religious will also grow in their own particular mission and charisms.

Conclusion

In conclusion, I now state concisely my basic premise which I have attempted to illustrate from a number of perspectives, and offer several brief recommendations:

1. The decline in number of candidates to the vowed life is strongly linked to the serious efforts toward renewal of women and men religious. However, the causal relationship we observe is related to the more secondary side-effects of this renewal which have been experienced more negatively than positively by many within and outside religious life.

It is essential that efforts at renewal of life, prayer and mission continue and deepen on the part of religious. We are now experiencing concrete fruits of that renewal and a renewed identification with a new generation of young and middle-age adults.

2. I believe that it is important for religious communities to accept the reality of fewer members now, and most proba-

bly in the foreseeable future. A definite choosing of this reality of being a "remnant" and the ramifications of this for life and ministry will free the members from much anxiety and enable them to plunge more earnestly into renewed life and mission.

3. On the other hand, there is much work to be done on the part of religious and others in the church to challenge and support the calls that are being given by God at the present time:

— renewed attitudes and programs supporting and encouraging minority candidates (in addition to members of racial minorities, there are divorced, widowed, chemically dependent, disabled and homosexual persons);
— developing and providing community structures and personnel to support and assist new members in their discernment and incorporation into community;
— increasing communication and education among all in order to help motivate them to promote the consideration of religious life vocations;
— working together to strengthen and develop all church vocations, especially those of the laity;
— encouraging and challenging church leadership to be active in dialogue with women and religious, and to continue ways to combat ingrained attitudes of clericalism and sexism.

Notes

1. Flannery, Austin, O.P. (ed.). *Vatican Council II: The Conciliar and Post Conciliar Documents.* Collegeville, MN: The Liturgical Press, 1975, p. 612.

2. Boelen, Bernard J. "Personal Maturity and the Christian Family."

3. Neal, Marie Augusta, SND deN. *Catholic Sisters in Transition: From the 1960s to the 1980s.* Wilmington, DE: Michael Glazier, Inc., 1984.

Shields, Joseph J., and Verdieck, Mary J. *Religious Life in the United States: The Experience of Men's Communities.* Washington, D.C.: CARA, 1985.

For sets of statistics, also consult the following: Ferry, K.M., Hoge, D.R., Potvin, R.H. *Research on Men's Vocations to Priesthood and Religious Life.* Washington, D.C.: USCC, 1984. Foundations and Donors Interested in Catholic Activities, Inc. (FADICA). *Laborers for the Vineyard: Proceedings of a Conference on Church Vocations.* Washington, D.C.: USCC, 1984.

McCready, William, and Sarther, Catherine. *Vocation Decisions; A Comparison Between Women Who Decided to Enter and Those Who Decided Not to Enter a Canonical Religious Community.* Chicago, IL: National Sisters Vocation Conference, 1983.

McCready, W., Sarther, C., Wemhoff, G. *Women in Religious Communities.* Chicago, IL: NSVC, 1981.

4. Op.cit., note #1, p. 396.

5. Hoge, Dean R. "Attitudes of Catholic College Students toward Vocations and Lay Ministry." Unpublished research, 1985.

The Contexts of Comings and Goings

John W. Padberg, S.J.

In 1385, the great western schism was tearing the church apart.

In 1485, Innocent VIII, one of the (several) less-than-edifying popes of the renaissance, was publicly arranging the sumptuous marriage banquets of one of his bastard children.

In 1585, Europe was about halfway through the religious wars which alternately smoldered and burst into flame over a period of more than a century and a quarter.

In 1685, Louis XIV revoked the Edict of Nantes, and in the name of the true faith persecuted the Huguenots of France.

In 1785, an exhausted church faced the enlightenment with seemingly little to say, and the revolution only four years away.

In 1885, the pope had already been a "prisoner of the Vatican" for fifteen years, and the church was only beginning to think of how it might address the world of the industrial revolution.

That is the way Jean Delumeau, the historian, responded when asked in 1985 to put some perspective on the present experiences in the church.[1]

The reflections that follow are those of an historian, too. They come in response to the invitation from the Pontifical Commission on Religious Life in the United States which asked for comments on two issues: why those who left religious life in the United States during the past two decades did

19

so and why young people are not entering religious congregations today in greater numbers.

As an historian, I judge that my best contribution to that invitation would be to put these particular phenomena into a context more extended in time than specific events occupying our attention today. First, I shall deal briefly with the three major periods of upheaval in religious life in the modern church. Second, I shall point out what happened to religious life in those three periods. Third, I shall note some of the special, or particular, characteristics of our present renewal. Finally, I shall note what seem to me to be some of the background reasons for the exodus from, and the non-entry into, religious life in the United States today. I'll make those observations, inevitably, in the light of my own experience, both personal (forty years as a religious) and professional (twenty years as a teacher and the last ten as administrator of a school of theology of the Society of Jesus).

Religious life in the church in the west has experienced major periods of upheaval three times in the last four hundred and fifty years: during the reformation (beginning in 1517), the French revolution (beginning in 1789), and in the renewal which was asked for in the aftermath of the Second Vatican Council, which ended in 1965.

The Reformation

The whole notion of religious life was rejected by Luther and Calvin and other Protestant reformers. This rejection had its foundation in the theology of the reformers, but it gained much of its popular support because of the scandalous reputation of many religious—especially male religious—and it was a reputation all too often deserved. Religious life had lost much of its credibility. One does not have to read Chaucer (before the reformation) or Rabelais (during it) for examples of this;

the documents of the church in those years, calling for reform, are vivid enough. Over and over those calls for reform were made, and over and over again they were ignored.

The effects on religious life in the lands of reform were devastating. Monks and nuns left their orders in droves. In England they were brutally thrown out of their houses. All of Scandinavia was lost to Rome, and Poland came very near being lost. Even in lands that stayed Catholic, the numbers of persons entering religious life dropped drastically. So bad had the reputation of religious life become that more than once it was proposed to the Holy See that all but four orders of men, and most orders of women, be suppressed.

And yet, in the midst of this seemingly impossible situation, the Catholic reformation took root and spread. New orders and congregations did arise, grew in numbers, and flourished. Older orders gradually took themselves in hand, reformed, and prospered.

The French Revolution

The French revolution brought chaos to the church and to religious life. Europe was the home of most of the members of the church. It was the place where the administrative structures, the financial resources, the educational establishments and charitable apostolates, the seminaries, the religious congregations, had been building for more than fifteen hundred years, all in aid of the preaching of the gospel and the celebration of the sacraments.

Quite simply, the revolution swept most of these away. For example, the lands upon which many of the dioceses and orders had depended for support were secularized by the new governments and sold to the highest bidder. (Cluny, the acme of Romanesque architecture, the glory of the Benedictine Order, the second largest church in the Christian world, was

21

destroyed—in small part by revolutionary frenzy, but in most part by several good middle class families who bought it from the state and had it taken down, stone by stone, the stones being sold to their profit for building material.)

Many of the religious orders were officially abolished in the lands reached by the revolution: members of almost all of them were turned out of their houses, and left to fend for themselves. In 1789, as the French revolution began, there were some two thousand Benedictine establishments in Europe; by 1815 only twenty were still functioning. In fact, of the many religious orders of men in existence before the French revolution, none except two—the Christian Brothers and the Jesuits—has ever again grown to be as large or larger in numbers as they were before the revolution.

And yet, the hundred and fifty years from the revolution to the beginning of Vatican II were, for religious congregations and orders, the most unusual years in the history of the church. More new congregations were founded than in any comparable period in the history of the church. More new congregations of women were founded in that century and a half than in the whole previous history of the church. The older orders grew again, in numbers and vitality. More missionary congregations were founded than ever before, and more women and men went to the foreign missions.

The Second Vatican Council

To turn now to our own histories, the Second Vatican Council brought undreamt of change to the church and to religious life. Many in the church had hoped for change, but no one could have imagined the depth and breadth of the change which did occur.

This is not the place to rehearse the events of the past twenty years. Perhaps, however, the quantity and especially the quality of that change can be evoked by recalling ten words and phrases from Vatican II. With two exceptions, none had been common in the church before the council:

> Aggiornamento
> Collegiality
> Dialogue
> People of God
> Lumen Gentium
> Inculturation
> Liturgy
> Religious Freedom
> Gaudium et Spes
> Ecumenism
> Revelation

Aggiornamento was symbolic of all the hopes aroused by the announcement of the council, of the changes made after the council, and of the debates over the interpretation of the council.

Collegiality, fundamentally an expression of the mutual relationships of the authority of bishops and pope, moved beyond that to become a way of expressing one of the aspects of all authority in the church.

Dialogue took its origin in the way that the Catholic Church was to relate to other Christian churches, but it soon was seen as a function that should characterize encounters internal to the church as well.

The *people of God,* a phrase with its roots in the Old Testament, and used in *Lumen Gentium* to describe the inner mystery of the church itself, now has taken on the resonance of a community that is varied, where each part of the community sustains the others on the pilgrim march into the future.

Inculturation meant the insertion of the experience of the faith into the very midst of the culture and mentality of a people. It is a concept that has changed the perspective with which evangelization takes place, and argues for a Christianity no longer normatively western but rather one taking flesh in a diversity of cultures.

Liturgy, a word and a renewal antecedent to the council, was perhaps the most visible, and to some the most disturbing, change, for it touched us all directly in our prayer and especially in the central continuing gestures of Christ, the sacraments of the church.

Religious Freedom became for the first time a part of church teaching, reversing previous official church positions, closing centuries of official intolerance and recognizing imprescriptible rights of the person. *Gaudium et Spes,* joy and hope, were the first words used to describe the fundamental way in which the church viewed the world as, for the first time in its history, it took up at a general council urgent secular questions of the day.

Ecumenism told us that we Christians were strangers no longer in our tragically separated churches, but sisters and brothers in Christ, with the duty and the privilege of seeking the way to the unity he prayed for. *Revelation* took us to scripture—lived out in the tradition of the community of the church as the way in which we came to know God's word and lived it out in the signs of the times—a stimulus to the renewal of teaching in scripture and in religious education throughout the church.

Perhaps men and women religious have been touched more than others by these words, and by the documents of Vatican II, because they were asked explicitly so soon after the council to review and revise their way of life in the light of the council's teachings. Their fundamental documents, their prayers, their manner of living, their apostolates, their communities—all came under scrutiny, often at great personal and institutional cost. And this was being done at a time during the 1960s and 1970s when the whole world was caught up in a series of extraordinary social and cultural changes.

While all this was going on, the number of people entering religious congregations began to drop dramatically, and the exodus of present members from the congregations began to rise drastically.

And yet . . .

An obvious and long-lasting turnaround in this most recent upheaval is, at present, only a possibility for the future. We are too close to the upheaval to expect an immediate turnaround in the number of entrants. At the same time, the exodus of those from the religious life seems to have slowed significantly. We can't draw more conclusions yet, for in this third example of upheaval we are no longer recounting history but immersed in events of the present.

Particulars of the Present

The renewal following Vatican II differs from that following the reformation and the revolution in that the recent upheaval took place *within* the church itself. Renewal has taken place inside the church; it came about at the desire of the church, as a result of its activities at Vatican II, fundamentally with its blessing and sometimes to its puzzlement or dismay. Renewal after Vatican II is a church-initiated activity, internal to its life. Nothing quite like it has ever happened before. No wonder we are sometimes puzzled by it.

Second, the renewal has been taking place in a context of rising expectations within the church itself. And, as any student of major changes realizes, such rising expectations have a tendency to outdistance realistic possibilities.

Third, the renewal of religious life has been taking place at the same time that a whole gamut of alternative possibilities for personal, dedicated service have appeared on the scene, beginning with the Peace Corps and going on to the Volunteer Corps of various religious orders. These alternative service possibilities also ask a commitment, give formation, provide a corporate endeavor, and foster a community life. Previously, for a Catholic, such dedicated service almost always involved long-term or lifetime commitment to a religious order. Today it is possible for the young man or woman to consider alternative ways to serve others and the Lord apart from the religious life.

Fourth, as Walter Kaspar, the theologian and secretary of the special synod of bishops, has noted, the years following Vatican II chanced to coincide with "a kind of cultural revolution which led to a break with tradition, a crisis of authority, an indifference toward questions of faith, great uncertainty about moral values, and a crisis in the realm of ethics."[2]

All of the factors we have been discussing so far have been external to religious life. The world, at the time of the reformation, the French revolution, and the Second Vatican Council, was in upheaval. A new religious culture, and a new way of conceiving the Christian life, was coming on the scene. Social changes took place more rapidly than they could be easily absorbed. In such circumstances the meaning of religious life in the church became unclear.

Let's now turn our attention to some of the factors internal to religious life in the United States that at present, it seems to me, are reasons for the lack of vocations and decline in numbers in religious congregations.

Why People Leave

1. <u>Loss of Corporate Identity</u>. The diminishment (perhaps, in some cases, a loss) of corporate identity by religious

communities seems to me to be the first and most important reason for the lack of vocations. There is little reason for a person to make and keep a lifelong, total commitment to a community if the community cannot make clear to itself and its members what it is, where it is going, and why. Certain congregations, either by definition or by long and seemingly inviolable custom, have been committed to one particular apostolate or one particular lifestyle, all inextricably embodied in constitution, rules and customs spelled out in detail with all the complex minutiae of a customs book. When much or all of that changes, it takes a long time for the congregation to forge a new corporate personality, and sometimes it is impossible.

2. <u>External regulations, imposed without regard to the internal dynamics of the community.</u> When new apostolates are taken on, it takes time for the community to structure them into itself by their very activity, and by reflection upon that activity. Such works have to seep into the community, pervade the rule of the congregation, its internal life, its shared vocabulary, its *sensibilité*. That is one reason why the recent statement by the Vatican Congregation for Religious and Secular Institutes that experimentation is at an end, and the report that the same Congregation is insisting upon greater uniformity in the constitutions presented to it for approval, may be unwisely cutting short a process that must have time.

3. <u>Disillusionment with actions of church officials.</u> The credibility of the church is called into question for many religious in the United States by some of the activities of church authorities. Even though someone genuinely realizes that to follow Christ is to partake both of his joys and his sorrows, it is not ordinarily going to be possible to do so without extraordinary graces (and no one has the right to presume such graces), if those who are supposed to be among Christ's representatives in the church appear to be acting in contrast, if not in down-

right opposition, to what the church itself has said so very recently. This lack of credibility in the words and deeds of some church officials—quite frankly, especially in the Roman curia—is one of the reasons for the problem of retention and recruitment.

4. Disillusionment with outmoded structures and activities of religious congregations. The credibility of religious orders sometimes has been damaged by faults in their own structures and activities. Outmoded practices and archaic rules, picayune procedures and loveless communities, are not calculated to retain old members or gain new ones. It is going to be hard for a young man or woman even to begin to think seriously of giving himself or herself to a religious life when religious communities are portrayed in the media as being populated by tyrannical monsters or—perhaps worse—by simpering, feckless featherbrains!

5. Alienation caused by some of the present teachings of the church, the theology upon which they are based, and the discipline with which they are enforced. An example of this is the present church teaching and discipline against the ordination of women. Some women religious may wish to be ordained, some may not. But a great many men and women, even with the best of will, cannot find convincing the present policy or the reasons alleged for it—reasons which have serious problems on several counts.

Credibility is strained when, even in circumstances in which everyone agrees that the priesthood is not involved, there is so little evidence that women religious are part of the process of framing questions, sharing consultations, and making decisions in the church.

6. Concern over social justice in relation to the religious life. The impetus to social justice and social activity by religious comes from Vatican II, from subsequent papal statements, from the proceedings of the Latin American Confer-

28

ence of Bishops meeting at Medellín, from liberation theology, and—often very vividly—from the direct experiences of religious women and men in encountering injustice and other social evils as they work to preach the gospel and redeem the world.

"Preach the gospel" and "redeem the world" have always been two heady concepts and two energizing goals. For religious today it is especially difficult to put social action and religious life together, because the vigorous social concern and activity of religious in the world today are, in part, a reaction against their exaggerated flight from the world in the past. When the pendulum swings so broadly exaggerations are almost inevitable. But at least the pendulum is swinging, and not at static rest.

Concluding Reflections: American Contexts and Shared Experience

Regardless of how we describe the situation in religious life in the United States today, and no matter what we think is to be done about it, the description, the thought, and the recommendations will have to be made in the context of what makes up this American people in an American tradition. Alexis de Tocqueville's *Democracy in America* is still worth more in gaining an insight into American character in general and religion in the United States than almost anything else one can read. It bears reading again.

A much more recent book, *Habits of the Heart*, by Robert Bellah et al., is an attempt to pick out and understand the central strands of the American tradition—the habits and mores that consciously and unconsciously inform our individual and communal lives as Americans, our private and public decisions. Bellah and his associates see four central strands: biblical, republican, utilitarian individualist, and expressive individualist.

Regarding the two individualist strands, the utilitarian individualist wants to push to the maximum the self-interest of the individual, while the expressive individualist sees every person as a "unique core of feelings variously expressed."

The authors suggest that the culture yields two poles of religion if the individualist strands are dominant in moral discourse. In the one "God becomes thoroughly external to our world," and in the other "God becomes self-magnified." With the biblical strand dominant, a covenanted communal relationship with God becomes evident; with the republican strand dominant, self-governance of equals may make for acute sensitivity to external or arbitrary incursions into the lives of those so governed.[3]

The implications are evident for those who are attracted to religious life in the United States today; for those who want to enter, stay in, leave; for those who are simply indifferent. We do not escape our culture. We should seek to Christianize it. American culture and Christianity will inevitably share with each other certain characteristics particular to themselves. And on that note, these remarks will end.

Cardinal Wojtyla, now Pope John Paul II, is quoted as having said in 1969 that conformism means death for any community, and that loyal opposition is necessary in any community. In the community of the universal church, loyalty has been a constant attitude; opposition, because of such loyalty, has been an infrequent position. But neither loyalty nor opposition, neither large numbers nor small, neither stability nor exodus can be ends in themselves. They are for the sake of that community itself, which is the church, the body of Christ. We are part of it. We have to share our experience of it with each other, with the universal church, with those who bear responsibility in the church.

Why? Because a living religion—or rather a religion which hopes to share its life—cannot ultimately afford to avoid the critical test of shared experience. On the contrary, from shared experience comes its life.[4]

The sections of this chapter which dealt with the reformation and the French revolution were each followed by a paragraph beginning, "And yet . . ." There followed a description of the revival of religious life—a revival that could almost be regarded as totally unexpected in the light of the terrible changes of the preceding decades.

It is too early to tell if we are in a similar revival of religious life after the changes of the renewal years. But when such a revival comes (or if it is even now being silently prepared) it will surely include, as it did in previous centuries, leaders of vision, communities of memory, corporate identities, apostolates shaped to a changed world, a church so credible that it gains once again an enthusiastic love, and the shared experiences of history, actuality, members' hopes, and plans for a future that goes beyond even 2085.

Notes

1. See Jean Delumeau in *Le Monde:* Aujourd'hui, November 17–18, 1985.

2. Walter Kaspar, Papers for German Bishops Preparatory to the Extraordinary Synod.

3. Robert Bellah, et al., *Habits of the Heart: Individualism and Commitment in American Life.* Berkeley: University of California Press, 1985.

4. William Barry, S.J., quoting John E. Smith in *The Tablet,* 239, 7581 (October 26, 1985), p. 1122.

A Look at the Institution Itself

James Hennesey, S.J.

The late Karl Rahner liked to remind his listeners that nothing created is absolute, only God.[1] That's a good starting point for an historical discussion of religious life and the point to which it has come. What I would like to contribute here is something of an historical overview of religious life in the United States—and to suggest that nothing created, even this, is absolute.

History deals with change. No change, no history. Change means that things were not always in the past as they are now, nor will they necessarily be in the future as they have been in the present or the past. All of this is, of course, a truism, easily seen when a given change-process has been completed. The difficulty—another truism—is for those caught somewhere along the line of change. And that last state is precisely where we most often find ourselves, or at least think we find ourselves. Some future historian may come along and decide that 1985 or 1986 was *the* year when a new age dawned. But that's not the way we see it—no more than those remote ancestors of ours thought that they were living in the "dark" or "middle" ages. No. We're somewhere in the middle, and we don't see the dimensions of change clearly. Forms we've inherited still have a normative hue about them, and new forms are still too nebulous.

The point I would like to make is that in addition to psychological, sociological and other profiles of current and ex-members of our religious communities, we should also take a look at the institution of religious life itself, particularly as it has developed in the United States.

My thesis is that we have in our country a classic instance of response to need as explanatory of (1) the development and growth of religious life, and (2) the present hiatus.

John Carroll, our first bishop, set the pattern. He wanted religious communities, both of women and men, for institutional service. Finding his ex-Jesuit brethren nestling on their parochial farms in southern Maryland unwilling to contribute to the projected academy at Georgetown, he reminded them sharply that their society had "rendered no service more extensively useful than that of education." When he learned that contemplative Carmelites were coming as the first women's community in Maryland, he was frank: "I wish rather for Ursulines." Schools were to become one of the spinal cords around which religious life in the United States developed. Hospitals became another, although not in Carroll's time.

There were other American specialties. Male religious communities brought their own particular devotions with them, and they were the backbone of the parish mission movement. But, to an extent unknown in Europe, they were advised from the beginning that parish work, whether in parishes for which they would have to assume corporate responsibility or as auxiliaries to the diocesan clergy, was expected. It was a need of the church to which they had to respond, not always with the most salutary effects on common life and regular observance. The non-parochial "public churches" of religious orders dot Europe's streets and squares. Not so in the United States. American religious have long been pastors, a charge for the most part confided only relatively recently to their European brethren.

American Catholics shaped a highly complex, highly institutionalized church. In part they responded to civic need, in part to what they perceived as their own religious needs in a nation both religiously and ethnically pluralistic. Controversies over Bible-reading, hymn-sings, and the generally Protestant tone of public schools led to the massive effort to have a parochial school in every parish. As Protestantism faded in the common schools, Catholics continued their parallel structure, now with secularism as the opponent.[2] Hospitals and other social, health and custodial-care institutions came into being, sometimes in response to civic need, sometimes in reaction to the proselytism which characterized public facilities.[3]

Members of religious communities in the United States became pre-eminently the servants of the church's institutions. Their bodies and lives made the institutions work. The church in the United States developed in its own unique way, creating institutions parallel to and frequently duplicating those of the state. In the process American religious became different. To give some examples: since the French revolution members of religious communities, except on an occasional individual basis, have scarcely engaged in university-level work in Europe. In the United States, men and women religious have founded, funded and administered well over two hundred university-level colleges. Agonies went into it, but now the educational level of American sisters places them as a group among the best-schooled women in the nation. American Catholic hospitals, now in many places moving into health-care systems, developed into sophisticated facilities demanding a high degree of management skills and technical training and competence in the religious who worked in them.

One factor which has affected the vocation/retention picture is surely the demand for professionalization. The options for ministry available to the religious generalist have narrowed. As that realization sinks in, it can cause community problems. "Professional" can be made to sound like a dirty word, antithetic to true religious spirit. But the reality remains. The days are gone when two or three religious letters after one's name might substitute for academic, professional or technical credentials. On the other hand, how many are called, willing and able to work out their religious vocation in and through a serious professional commitment, whatever their field? And how many are willing to do it if the domestic atmosphere in which it must be done is not supportive?

A problem lurking down deep in the debate just noted is the "instrumental" character of the religious man's or woman's commitment to one or the other professional track. My being a historian, her being a physicist, we see it as a way of fulfilling our religious vocation. That has become increasingly difficult as we work in hospitals or schools which are no longer manageable as extensions of our religious community. Size, sophistication and government funding have made them new entities. We compete for jobs, we are promoted, we are fired. It is a very new religious vocation. The institutionalization of the church in the United States grew in response to the perceived needs of the nineteenth and early twentieth centuries. To what need does my new vocation respond? To what extent is it vitiated as a religious vocation by the fact that it brings in a substantial salary, welcome in a time when old-age security has become a preoccupation, and not only of seculars. What does it all say to the attractiveness of a religious vocation?

But neither do I believe the alternative is the answer. There are communities that resolutely resist the changing times. We have little data on them. The impression is that vocationally they do well. It would not be surprising. But the lesson of history is against them. Ultimately religious life lives—indeed with its particular charism, but contemporary with its times—or it withers.

We most often find ourselves "somewhere along the line of change." That is where we American religious are now. The super-institutionalized church of our youth (or the youth of some of us) had begun to play itself out by the mid-1960s. Colleges began down the road to autonomy. High school and grammar school classrooms seemed less attractive than more direct social action. Hospitals moved ever more firmly under the twin thumbs of government bureaucrats and insurers. Government jobs—various kinds of public service—opened up. So did what might be called "para-community" organizations, the volunteer corps attached to several religious communities—not to mention the Peace Corps, VISTA and the like. Religious were attracted out of communities. Or, remaining in communities, they were allowed or encouraged to take secular employment. And there were attractive alternatives for some who might otherwise have considered religious life—alternatives less permanent, less confining, less entangled in recondite canonical legalities. Educated young people who have been encouraged to take control of their own lives, to consider the wide range of options open to them and to make responsible choices are unlikely to enlist in an organization whose members—in all too painful specific instances—they see being dealt with by an impersonal, distant bureaucracy which presumes it has control of their lives.

Other factors can be multiplied. We have been passing through a world period of enormous socio-cultural change. Neither the church nor religious communities within the church have been exempt from that reality. Since the Second World War, the American Catholic community has changed radically. It has moved up startlingly in social and economic scales. One result has been the community's suburbanization, to which too little attention has yet been paid. The economic success that made the phenomenon possible is, of course, one topic that must be considered. What consequences have there been which bear on the subject of religious vocation? There is something else also. The very nature of the suburban community has meant that many young Catholics grow up without coming into contact with religious priests, sisters or brothers. We are not part of—or at best a relatively marginal part of—their parish life. We are seldom part of their school life. We scarcely exist for them.

Someone better versed than I will have to address another question. There are still many Catholics in the cities. Some are in gentrified areas, some in old, often still ethnic neighborhoods. Others are blacks or Hispanics. A whole new generation of immigrant Catholics continues to arrive from many countries. Our black bishops have recently reminded us how "white European" our church is; others find it "Anglo." It is obviously a problem for religious communities. How do religious communities respond to these new people with new needs? Is their response such that they are likely to attract candidates to share in that response? The litany can go on and on.

But enough. I am not sure that we are right to ask why vocations are declining—or some variant of that. Another way to phrase the question is to ask what need there is for X or Y religious community in a given segment of the church. Is there a need? What services does the community render to the people of God of the local church or to other parts of the church universal that justify it in seeking candidates? Obviously, there are imperative demands in justice on the church to care for its aging and sick religious. I would be prepared to argue for a system of equitable sharing of resources. But that is not at issue here, though it must be elsewhere. Neither am I prepared at this juncture in history to contemplate the imminent demise of religious community as one of the possible ways of Christian living.

My conclusion, from my study of history, is that religious institutes will prosper only when there is a real sense among God's people that collectively and individually, by the way they live and pray together and by the contribution they make to the commonweal, they respond to deeply felt needs within the Christian body. When religious devote themselves to bitter-sweet nostalgia for a past beyond recall and to preoccupation with their own secure survival, the only future is further decline.

It need not, of course, be so.

Two vignettes have stayed with me ever since I first read them. One is in A. G. Dickens' fine book, *The English Reformation*.[4] Discussing the pathetic situation of the English monasteries on the eve of their dissolution at the hands of Henry VIII and his agent Thomas Cromwell, he points out that there were noble exceptions, but that the general picture was that of "an uninspired and lukewarm establishment" which fell like ripe fruit to the despoilers. John McManners drew the second picture in *The French Revolution and the Church*,[5] of the sloth and preoccupation with material possessions too typical of many of the male religious of 1789, men who lived "in the drowsy *bonhomie* of isolated religious clubs," and had lost all sense of service. It obviously need not have been that way, either in the England of the sixteenth century or the France of the eighteenth century.

Both moments were followed by catastrophe. But after that came, in the first instance, the counter-reformation flowering of communities of apostolic service and, in the second, the nineteenth century Catholic revival in which so many communities were born and so many born again.

The shape of the times to come, and our ability and freedom to respond to them, hold the answer to what will be the newest incarnation of the ideals of the founders and foundresses of religious communities throughout the ages.

Notes

1. See, for example, Karl Rahner, S.J., "And What Do You Think?" *The Jesuits: Yearbook of the Society of Jesus 1974–1975* (Rome, 1974), p. 32.

2. Harold J. Buetow, *Of Singular Benefit: The Story of U.S. Catholic Education* (New York, 1970).

3. James Hennesey, S.J., address to the Catholic Health Association of the United States, Orlando, FL, June 4, 1985, excerpted in *Hospital Progress* 66 (November 1985), pp. 28–29, 56.

4. A.G. Dickens, *The English Reformation* (London, 1967), pp. 80–89.

5. John McManners, *The French Revolution and the Church* (New York, 1969), pp. 8–9.

The Vocation Crisis:

Reflections on and Approaches to the Data

Howard J. Gray, S.J.

In the two questions concerning religious life—why they left and why more are not entering—the presumption is that there is something to remedy in the U.S. church situation, and that, if remedied, vocations to religious life would increase and stabilize. To some degree I share this presumption. However, after having reflected both on the Neal and CARA studies, and then on my own experiences as a formation director, theological school rector and dean—and more recently as a major superior—I also wondered whether some consideration ought not to be directed more positively toward what God might be revealing and inviting us to accept and to act upon.

Suppose that we ask: What is God saying to us about the direction this United States vocational phenomenon is taking? It is this possibility, of revelation and direction, which I would like to explore from the viewpoint of spiritual theology. By spiritual theology I mean the effort to discern and to articulate systematically the movement of God's Spirit in creation, covenant, and Christ—and the continuing labor for life, community, and discipleship which the Spirit inspires and sustains in the experience of men and women of committed Christian faith.

I have organized my reflections under three headings: Acknowledging the Data, Discerning the Possible Good, and Some Decisions for Future Action.

Acknowledging the Data

The data which both the Neal and CARA studies provided is clear but limited. It is clear that men and women, generally, leave religious life because they do not find in it the affective satisfaction which they feel, think, or believe they have the right to experience. It is clear that assigning specific reasons why people are not entering religious life is going to be a hypothetical venture. Finally, it is also clear that both of these studies, although invaluable, invite further research— that is, both studies have limitations. From the viewpoint of spiritual theology, I would say that there are at least five possible contrasting interpretations of the data. Let me play with these five possible interpretations:

A. *People leave religious life today because:*

1. They are not affectively satisfied—which is another way of saying that they do not understand, or, understanding, they do not accept the hard reality of the cross, namely, that they are disciples of a Lord who confirmed his love for the human by laying down his life for others, a climactic act of humiliation, forgiveness, and self-donation which forever reveals the real test of love: to put aside one's reputation, convenience, pleasure, dreams, and lesser loves to accept the burden of loving in self-donation as Christ did.

2. They are not affectively satisfied—which is another way of saying that people have come to realize the true meaning of the cross, i.e. a witness to the power of love and self-donation to lead to the freedom of the resurrection where joy and life confirm that in this suffering God is present. These people may have left religious life because, in true humility, they found that God was not in their suffering and now called them to another form of self-donation in a sacrifice which leads to their participation in the resurrection of Christ.

B. *People do not enter religious life because:*

1. Modern culture, particularly in the U.S., is antithetical to Christian values: hedonistic, narcissistic, restless, competitive, and absorbed by and with economic prestige and professional viability. Consequently, it is hard for young people or single professionals to disengage themselves from this mind-set and value system and to consider seriously the kind of life symbolized by the vows. Religious life must represent an unambiguous dedication to God's revelation and an unambiguous opposition to the world's self-dramatization and pseudo-values.

2. Our modern culture, especially in the U.S., despite its pervasive secularism and frequently articulated religious indifference, is the cultural-social reality in which God challenges us especially to the mission of peace, justice, and the establishment of a human community of mutual concern and even love. Too frequently, religious professionals represent either a withdrawal from cultural and social realities or a capitulation to that reality. Consequently, young people do not feel drawn to this way of life. Religious life must represent a consecration for a mission which seeks faith but is expressed in works of peace, justice, and the establishment of true human community.

C. *People do not enter religious life and people leave religious life today because:*

1. The U.S. church has been torn apart by or struggled with or was caught in conflicting views of what its identity and mission are. People cannot peacefully pursue their reli-

2. The U.S. church has been compromised by its confusion of mission with maintenance. On the one hand, the bishops have spoken out on the overriding mission of peace, justice,

.gious life nor focus well their apostolic talents in a climate of such ambiguity and conflict. Moreover, people are not going to be drawn to give their lives to a local church so confused and so disunited. The kingdom of God demands a church clear in its self-definition and united in its mission. Orthodoxy and orthopraxis are, ultimately, the issues and the primary responsibility of episcopal leadership. When the leaders themselves are clear and in union, then vocations will flourish.

and the creation of true human community. On the other hand, bishops—on a day-to-day basis—spend a tremendous amount of energy on pleasing and assuring those who want Catholicism to support unequivocally U.S. economic prosperity, the status quo in our use of church buildings, resources, and man/woman power. A caretaker church will not attract nor keep those who feel that the kingdom should define the church, not the church the kingdom. For these kinds of people, religious life can seem to represent a church intent more on maintenance than on mission.

D. *People do not enter religious life and people leave religious life today because:*

1. Religious communities, whose leadership has been dominated by doctrinaire liberals, have abandoned the symbols, discipline, and concentrated mission which, in the past, gave them clear identity and specific purpose. If someone sees that religious are like any other good but not consecrated Christians

2. Religious communities have been in a period of intense refocusing of their identity, discipline, and mission, a period which found many religious unprepared to deal with ambiguity and change. Within this ambiguity, two trends seem to have emerged:
a. one which views religious

or, even worse, if someone sees that religious are increasingly secular, each doing his or her own thing, then of course people will neither enter religious life nor endure in it.

community life, with its faith communication (prayer, worship, communal discernment, shared and expressed value system), as the primary apostolic witness of religious communities; therefore, the community is emphasized; and/or b. one which sees religious community life as supportive of apostolic commitment and even as an animator of apostolic discernment and action but as secondary to the work to be done by religious outside their community.

E. *People do not enter religious life and people leave religious life today because:*

1. The ability to be committed permanently to any person, institution, or cause has itself been seriously eroded in our times. There are many reasons for this: e.g. the breakdown of traditional family life and marriage, the swift changes in company ownerships which, in turn, inhibit sustained company loyalties, the highly mobile character of U.S. executives and their families so that the old notion of "neighbor-

2. The ability to be committed has shifted from "things" to persons-in-need. If religious communities could clearly commit themselves to the priority of meeting the needs of the marginated, the poor, the estranged in our society and in our church, then quality people would come and stay. At the same time, since people are also living longer, "permanence" in any kind of lifestyle or work is a relative reality. We have be-

hood" has died, the scandals of Watergate, Vietnam, and the easy assasinations of leaders. People cannot say "forever" because they have less and less experience of permanence in their lives. We need to regain a rock-bottom adherence to permanence in marriage, family, values, and, of course, religious and priestly lives. We have to challenge any effort to relax these kinds of commitments in order to regain that sense of "forever" which will make people stick to their promises.

come a two or even three career society. Perhaps we need to adapt the vows to this reality, not denying commitment but adjusting it to shorter-term expressions of that commitment. If religious life could be organized for less permanent commitments, there may be both a healthier community life and more realistic apostolic planning.

While I am confident that there are other categories of interpretation on why people leave or do not enter religious life, these five represent what I have read or heard as the major reasons. It is clear, too, that those reasons listed under column #1 represent a more conservative interpretation, while those reasons listed under column #2 represent a more liberal interpretation. However much we may deplore such classifications, they continue to have meaning as legitimate, if broad, classifications. That is all I intend here.

Discerning the Possible Good

Granted there is a need to remedy possible defects in U.S. religious life—we are, indeed, always called to reform and to renewal—I want to say a word for something good in the

45

phenomenon of fewer religious vocations. The good I see can fall under five headings:

A. United States religious-life leadership has been largely faithful to the essential directions and spirit of Vatican II. As a result, both the Leadership Conference of Women Religious (LCWR) and the Conference of Major Superiors of Men (CMSM) represent women and men who seriously and consistently promote evangelical values and prayer, a genuine concern for their respective charisms, and a commitment to meet generously the needs of the time—particularly the needs for justice, for peace, and the transformation of our society into a structure responsive to true human and Christian community.

B. In response to these fidelities, most of the U.S. religious who have entered and remained in religious life have experienced freedom and a high degree of personal accountability. There is a solid group of self-directed religious who have committed themselves to mature obedience and collaboration with their leadership.

C. The freedom to be authentic means a freedom to recognize the spurious vocation. Consequently withdrawal from religious life, no matter how extensive, does not necessarily mean defection from Christian life, Christian values, or Christian apostolic service. Painful as it is, it is still better to have people leave freely when they discover that they cannot lead the religious life happily and to redirect them into another style of Christian life and work.

D. The lessening of numbers should (could? will?) prompt us to examine far more creatively the ways that religious women and men could collaborate together, could eliminate needless apostolic duplication, could support both lay collaboration and lay co-determination, could plan for a better deployment of available personnel. In short, "thinking small" does not mean defeat but realignment.

E. Decreased membership in the face of ever-increasing

apostolic demands is a genuine problem for U.S. religious leadership. We must search for causes and remedies. However, the specific value of spiritual theology is that its hermeneutic is to discern the mystery within human experience, the action of God, and not just the problems to be analyzed and resolved. The present vocational reality could well represent a revelation which calls for obedience, new direction, and renewed religious fidelity to God's reality, not ours. The experience of lessened resources before great apostolic challenges is hardly alien to our religious tradition; from Abraham to Moses to Joshua to Gideon to Esther to Mary to Jesus to the early church, we have an ancestry marked more by need than by power. Let me explore what some possibilities might be if, indeed, this present vocational situation is the situation for a long time to come.

First, we have to accept our limitations as God's will, not God's displeasure. We have to begin to see our limitation as a gift, not a deprivation. Is there something which we could become if we saw ourselves called to be smaller in numbers? More prayerful? More trusting? More deeply charitably open to working with, to supporting, to relying on one another? Could not this openness to mutual support for the sake of the kingdom, in turn, open new apostolic possibilities of religious-lay colleagueship, of a church committed to preaching and teaching the universal, a church committed to holiness, apostolic service, and co-determination?

I am aware that the rhetoric of such collaboration has been with us for some time. I am aware, too, that we possess practical examples of such collaboration. What I am urging is that our vocational situation could be summoning us to plan for a church whose mission can only be fulfilled through a rich partnership of baptismal ministers.

Discerning the possible good is at least as important as discerning the possible defect. If one grants that there is solid evidence that U.S. religious have cooperated with the renewal prompted by Vatican II at least as much as they may have resisted or ignored it, then it seems reasonable and, even more, deeply Christian to resist an interpretation of the numerical decline of religious-life members which reduces the explanation simply to sinfulness on the part of religious or, at least, to their sustained poor judgment about renewal. It seems that we must be willing to examine the possibly positive significance behind the numerical decline, i.e. in part this may indicate God's call to the church to extend to all the baptized full ministerial holiness, service, and leadership. Let me pursue that possibility.

The church is a legitimate instrument of the kingdom of God, not its substitute. The means which the church has used to attain its finality, incorporation into God's kingdom, are means to an end. One of the chief means of the church's service of the kingdom is people committed to the direct ministry of the word, sacrament, and works of mercy. In our historical reality, a major contributor to that pool of committed people has been religious. Religious have preached, explained, researched the word; religious have administered, explained, researched the sacraments; religious have taught the poor and uneducated; religious have healed and helped Christians meet death; religious have confronted the haughty and unjust with the mercy of God's justice. What is important is that the ministry of the church at the service of God's kingdom has been an ongoing reality. What is historically true is that religious have been important, even indispensable, in the church's ministry. But that historical reality does not constitute an indispensable nor an exclusive means to the church's service of the kingdom.

Our times may well call us to accept the numerical decline of religious as God's invitation to understand and to implement practically and consistently the call of all baptized to be disciples. The future lies—perhaps—more in the intelligent yet humble effort we employ to make practically possible the universalization of discipleship in the Church. Religious women and men may decline but Christ's invitation endures. It is the church leadership which must facilitate lay women's and men's ability to answer that call and thus keep the Church's work for the Kingdom vibrant.

Some Decisions for Future Action

As a major religious superior I worry about the vocation issue on many levels:

Can I staff our present local, national, and international commitments with adequate, trained Jesuit professionals?

How do I get Jesuits to see collaboration with other religious and with lay colleagues and diocesan clergy as the normal mode of contemporary apostolic action?

How do I insure that young Jesuits be given time to mature in their apostolic personalities, resisting the pressures to put them in charge of works or communities before they have been given time to know success and failure in the ministry?

How do I help my province to keep religiously creative and professionally competent to assume specifically new ministries, particularly in direct social ministries in the U.S. and in emerging opportunities in the third world?

How do I communicate a vision for the future, for apostolic risk, for creative options, when as a matter of fact our membership is getting older and, understandably, tired?

Finally, what do I say in an integrated way about the findings set forth in the data of the Neal and CARA reports?

These concerns are not uniquely my own. For those called to serve as major superiors today these are some of our key problems. What I never have heard is anyone in religious leadership suggesting that we lower standards to meet personnel needs. We continue to ask for qualified women and men. Consequently, our first future direction should be to continue to articulate our understanding of our problems and to resist meeting these by lowering our admittance standards. We should be what our charisms have asked us to be.

Second, we should promote lay collaboration and lay co-determination in our apostolic works, in our formation, and in our planning.

Third, we should view decline with a tough-minded resolve to improve, to be converted, and to become more attuned to Christ's priorities—but also with a tough-minded resolve to accept our numerical reality and to organize ourselves for a new apostolic strategy based on inter-community/inter-diocesan collaboration. In brief, we should resist simplistic resolutions to tighten up discipline, to be preoccupied with intramural conventions, and to retreat to a kind of sectarianism which separates us from people and the world where they work and struggle.

In 1983, Philip Murnion said:

It seems to me that the call to vocations will be to the extent that the whole community and mission of

Christ are embodied in the people. To this extent, a Church can call people to ministry and the call can be heard, because it is being spoken by that whole body of the Church; the call can be heard by those who have been disposed to hear that call by the Spirit of God. It will be to the extent to which the Church as a whole body, living out its responsibility for vocations—making that vocation plausible and conveying that a vocation, as a call to a sacrifice, is pertinent to today's world—that we will again see some change in the vocation picture.[1]

This reflection comes close to what I want to offer here. There is, I feel, something graced for us in seeing the two questions about vocations (why they left and why more are not entering religious life) not only as problems, but as invitations to the church in the United States to enter into an era of conscious commitment to preaching, teaching, and leading its membership to full discipleship in and for the kingdom. This is the environment—and I believe the only environment—in which religious life in the future can and should be offered as one way of following Christ in his work for the kingdom of God.

Note

1. *Laborers for the Vineyard*, Proceedings of a Conference on Church Vocations, held December 1–2, 1983, at the Drake Hotel, Chicago, Illinois (Washington, D.C.: USCC, 1984), pp. 131–132.

What Meaning Do We Give to the Data?

Regina Bechtle, S.C.

I offer my remarks on the loss and decline in religious vocations among women in the United States with the realization that such a complex issue admits of no facile analysis, and that a claim to total perspective is but an optical illusion. My observations took shape in dialogue with other religious and need to be tested in continuing conversation with the members of the Christian community.

I will address some issues of hermeneutics: What meaning do we give to the data, and what biases and assumptions govern our interpretation?

What Is the Spirit Saying to the Church?

In any process of analysis, after data is collected and experience observed, one must eventually ask, "What does this information *mean?*" Documenting the *fact* of the loss/ decline of religious vocations is one step, probing its possible *causes* another, but grasping its *significance* is yet a third step.

What *might* the loss/decline be saying to us? That God no longer speaks to us and wishes to call people to religious life? That the life of the vows is no longer a way in which God may be found and God's reign served?

Religious to whom I put these questions chose rather to interpret the fact of declining numbers as a call and a challenge, and it is their belief that the present critical situation calls contemporary religious to:

☐ speak the truth of their lives to one another and to the world without hesitation or ambiguity.

☐ deepen their commitment to live at the heart of the gospel and in service to those most in need, even when this commitment leads to uncomfortable choices and unpopular stands.

☐ affirm, in theory and practice, an ecclesiology which recognizes that all Christians are consecrated and missioned in virtue of their baptism.

☐ live and work in interdependence among congregations, to collaborate with laity and clergy, to build networks with all who are living in truth and working for the reign of God.

☐ take on new roles in ministry, walking with, reflecting with, and empowering others, especially the laity.

☐ learn again to be servant, to be poor, to be without the power of numbers and prestige; to abandon attitudes of control or superiority over the lives of others.

And most fundamental is that the present state of attrition is seen as inviting us religious to yield our future to the designs of the Spirit and to follow the Lord along a path as yet unknown, trusting that God will not abandon us to death without the promise of life.

Each of us brings an interpretative framework, a bias, if you will, to the task of constructing meaning. In fact, as even contemporary science acknowledges, our biases are operative from the very beginning of our work, influencing what we notice and what we ignore. We have no access to uninterpreted, "purely objective" data. In other words, there are no neutral observers and reporters, no abstract facts without an interpreter and his or her commitment, out of which interpretation arises.

When believers describe experience, and still more when

they attempt to discern the meaning of that experience, they too bring a bias, a commitment. Many religious, including myself, would describe their bias as follows: First, we believe that the Spirit is indeed speaking through the events and circumstances of the present vocation crisis, even as we struggle to understand what the Spirit is saying. Second, we believe that the mission of Jesus, to reveal God's love and to establish God's reign, will endure, through whatever means are necessary to continue it. Religious life may undergo many mutations, or it may go out of existence entirely (though such is certainly not our hope), but at a fundamental level, that outcome is not our concern. Why should not Jesus' injunction to "seek first the kingdom of God" (Mt 6:33) guide the priorities of communities, congregations, and churches, as well as those of individual Christians?

Bringing one's interpretative bias to light is difficult enough. But to complicate the situation even further, one's choice to interpret data in one way and not another—one's "commitment"—rests on the still deeper level of *assumptions*. Such assumptions, or, in our context, statements of faith, express a foundational experience of God.

The respondents of my small sample, along with many other religious, affirm their faith in a Spirit who speaks today and in a mission that will endure. Out of what experience of God do such statements of faith arise? What is our experience of God's relationship to humankind, of the way God speaks to us and works in history, of where and how we have access to God? What does God want for us and of us? How do we discover it? What shape does it give to our life?

The interpretations and the causes of the loss/decline reflect a certain theological bias which arises out of a certain experience of God. Let me attempt to name that experience as follows:

1. At the heart of human life, we experience God as

present. Personal and societal life mediate God's activity in a real and privileged way.

2. At the heart of the human and divine reality, which is the *ecclesia*, we experience the communion of all its members, united in a common discipleship, sharing in a common consecration and mission by virtue of baptism.

3. At the heart of life we experience the inevitability of death. At the heart of the saving mystery of Jesus, the servant, we experience the paradox of his surrender to death, in trust that life and not destruction awaited him on the other side of death. At the heart of our existence as servant communities in a servant church, we are beginning to experience the mystery of death and the crucial nature of our corporate response to this mystery.

Much more could be said about each of the above aspects of God experience. Let me focus here on the last two.

Communion of Disciples in Consecration and Mission

The documents of Vatican II formally ended an era when the mission of the church was viewed as the responsibility solely of the hierarchy and clergy, consecrated or set apart by orders, and of religious, consecrated by the profession of the evangelical counsels.[1] Simultaneously, the church has been rediscovering the implications of baptism for consecration and mission.

To be baptized into Christ is to enter into a community set apart for mission, not for smug self-congratulation, nor for narcissism, nor for insulation from the world, but for the work of the gospel, for announcing the good news of the salvation which has come in Jesus Christ, the reign of God which has taken flesh in him and has begun in our midst. Christians are made holy, "consecrated," so that they may live out that consecration by being sent, as Jesus himself was sent from God. And Christians undertake the mission, whether of preaching, reconciling, healing, or performing works of mercy, only in Jesus' name, only in virtue of the consecration received in baptism.

The multiplication of lay vocations to service in our day, far from being an aberration or a stopgap measure useful only until priestly and religious vocations increase once more, brings us closer to what should be the normal state of the church, one in which all Christians are living out their baptismal consecration, taking responsibility for the life of the body of Christ and for its mission in the world.

What then is the relationship of religious consecration to baptismal consecration? How should we understand religious consecration in a way that is not elitist, that does not label it a higher, better, or superior form of Christian life, a guarantee of privileged access to God, but which yet affirms its distinctiveness as a Christian vocation?

Sandra Schneiders, whose contributions to a contemporary theology of religious life are well known, considers the "urgency" of this very question to be "a special grace of our historical situation." She approaches an answer by probing the dynamic of the incarnation, which mends the rift between sacred and profane realms and thus radically transforms our perspective on consecration. Schneiders writes:

> Humans need not be separated and made superior in order to mediate between earth and heaven; rather God became human, entered profoundly into solidarity with us, renounced divine inaccessibility and became our equal and our intimate, not just to bridge but to abolish the distance between God and humanity.[2]

She continues: "We do not need to set certain persons apart, to make them superior, so that they can gain entrance to a God from whom ordinary people must shrink."[3]

Schneiders locates the distinctiveness of religious vows in the particular shape they give to a Christian's baptismal consecration. She envisions the church as a community of "evangelical equality" where categories of superior and inferior no longer apply, where only one, God, is acknowledged as master and Lord, and where the servant's place, the lowest, is sought by all.

The Response of Religious Congregations to the Mystery of Death

"Those who would save their life will lose it; those who lose their life for my sake will save it" (Lk 9:24). Each of us knows the truth of these words of Jesus, bringing us face to face with a fundamental law of the reign of God.

Each of us has experienced how more and more of our energy can become absorbed in preserving, hoarding, increasing what we have, until it quite literally "has" us, holding us captive. The only way out is to give it over, all of it, all that we have to live on, whether that be the two copper coins of the widow in Luke's gospel, or the liberty, memory, understanding and will which form the core of our very selves.

Life in the Spirit operates according to the law of reversal: strength is discovered in weakness, joy in sorrow, finding in losing, life in death. The poetry of it all can obscure the cold, hard truth which Jesus embodied and to which believers have witnessed through the ages: the road to life leads through death. There is no detour.

Some try to short-circuit death by rebelling against it; some resign themselves to it in cowardice or bitterness. Still others see in Jesus one who became obedient to this ultimate mark of the human condition, even when it was inflicted upon him violently and unjustly.[4]

This parabolic logic of reversal, eminently true on the personal level of life in the Spirit, also applies, I suggest, to

Spirit-led communities.[5] Among them, over the past few decades, religious congregations have been giving up, voluntarily or involuntarily, much of what they formerly had to live on—certainties, securities, prestige, self-definition, stable and familiar forms of living and serving, respected institutional commitments, and, most painful of all, their most valuable resource, their members.

I do not mean to imply that either the loss of many members or the lack of large numbers entering today is the result of the deliberate choice of congregations. My point is simply that for us believers these phenomena cannot be interpreted without reference to their paschal connotations.

Grieving for what has been lost is certainly an appropriate response, much as one would grieve over the loss of a loved one, or as a couple might mourn its childlessness. But grief is not the last word, nor is death. For Christians, much as we resist death, we yet believe that it is the way to a fuller, more abundant life, a life that is not won or earned as a reward, a life that is not so much under our control as it is bestowed on us—the free gift of a loving God.

Many religious who have weathered the last two turbulent decades and have chosen to remain in religious life speak of a deepened awareness of their call. Fidelity to that experience of God's call has brought them and their congregations to this moment, a moment which looks for all the world like an advanced stage of terminal illness. It is no wonder that few others want to cast their lot with the dying!

Does this mean, then, that the call was an illusion, the response self-deception? Is the crisis in vocations a punishment of congregations for mistakes made, an indictment for something they have failed to do or have done inadequately? Or is this time of crisis in religious life a call to exchange, like Abraham, our dreams for God's, to assent, like Mary, to a destiny we would never have designed for ourselves, to choose fearfully, yet freely, like Jesus, to surrender our life to forces beyond our control? Are we being led by God where we would rather not go, into a situation of institutional impoverishment, corporate abandonment to the mystery of life through death? Perhaps the direction of the Spirit's leading is not yet as clear as I would like to think, but if God's ways prove not to be identical to ours, we ought not to be too surprised.

Notes

1. Cf., among many examples, *Lumen Gentium,* nos. 10–12, 30–35, 39–42; *Apostolicam Actuositatem* (Decree on the Apostolate of the Laity), nos. 2–4.

2. Sandra M. Schneiders, "Evangelical Equality: Religious Consecration, Mission, and Witness," Part II, *Spirituality Today* 39, 1 (Spring 1987), pp. 56–57 (quote from pp. 60–61).

3. Ibid., p. 61.

4. Leonardo Boff, "How Does One Preach the Cross Today in a Society of the Crucified?" Unpublished translation of article in *Christus* 49 (March–April 1984), pp. 27–33. Cf. his statement: ". . . we must reckon with the destiny of the Suffering Servant and with the price that Jesus paid. . . . There are moments—and Jesus lived such a one—in which only martyrdom and the sacrifice of one's own life do justice to life and preserve fidelity to the cause of God."

5. This same conclusion is developed from a sociological perspective by Lawrence Cada, S.M., et al., *Shaping the Coming Age of Religious Life* (New York: Seabury, 1979), which discusses the life cycle of religious groups.

Part Two

Factors of Change, Past and Present

Religious Life—1965-1985

Kristin Wombacher, O.P.

It is my belief that reflections on why those who left religious life did so should in large part depend on how one has come to understand/conceptualize what happened in religious life between 1965 and 1985. It would be possible for any professional from a particular discipline to read the data as given and identify trends. But to have lived within religious life for those twenty years and to have worked with a wide variety of religious during that period gives one a keen understanding of the phrase, "You had to be there." However, it is not just having had the experience of religious life during that time frame that is most influential. It is the conceptualization of what actually was happening that strongly shapes and colors one's reflections on "why those who left did so." Similarly, the experience and conceptualization of religious life, of the church, and of societal movements today will be strong determiners of how one reflects on the second issue of why young people today are not entering in greater numbers.

In trying to conceptualize what was happening in religious life from 1965 to 1985, I will look at the changes that took place from four different but related perspectives. *Perfectae Caritatis* serves as the starting point. It called for the adaptation and renewal of religious life which was to be centered on the following of Christ as proposed by the gospel and the spirit of the founder/foundress, and it was to include an adjustment to the changed conditions of the time. The wisdom of the Second Vatican Council urged women and men religious both to return to the gospel and their unique charism and to move out of the medieval cloister era into the contemporary world. In the imagery of John XXIII, the window was thrown open and the spirit of aggiornamento swept through.

Adaptations

And so religious began, hesitantly at first, modifications in daily practices, prayers, dress. A varied, shortened format of praying; modest, meager allowances on a trial basis; talking to one another outside formal recreation; modified veil, raised hemlines, colored shirts; changes in schedule; the excitement of going to K-Mart alone—these first changes were "adaptations." They seemed monumental at the time, but in fact these were the external changes requested and expected by Rome in terms of adapting to the contemporary needs and circumstances of our time and culture. While such adaptations were often more obvious because they were usually external and visible, they were really the least significant changes in themselves. Still these minor external adaptations opened more windows and led to many much more significant changes.

Maturation

Soon congregational chapters moved beyond the adaptations of externals to more substantive issues. They turned to writing identity statements. But everyone in the congregation was to be included. Polls, committees, questionnaires, position papers and proposals proliferated. That is, *individual* opinions were sought, ushering in the breakdown of what I have come to call the "herd mentality." To paraphrase the man-in-the-gray-flannel-suit, religious in the black/brown/ white habit were no longer a collective entity. This movement toward *individuality* occurred in other areas as well. Not planned, and in fact against the operating norms of the day, little by little religious began slipping away from institutional apostolates to other works. Also, the congregational summer retreat for hundreds gave way to private directed retreats and spiritual direction. In many ways the herd was out of the corral and wandering far and wide. In this first phase of the second process of change, the emphasis was on increasing *individuality* and becoming *self*.

In phase two, which was sometimes following, sometimes concurrent with, phase one, religious sought out and struggled to develop closeness, *intimacy*, and deep personal sharing. Some tried setting up small experimental living situations. But the struggle, whether in experimental houses, conventual houses, or the workplace, was for intimacy, depth sharing, and interpersonal closeness. And it was a painful struggle. Attempts were also made to introduce personal faith sharing into communal prayer. When not accepted in the local house, some religious formed faith-sharing prayer groups outside their living situation. And, with the onus of particular friendships dispelled, friendships within and without religious congregations flourished. Much of the focus during this phase two was on *intimacy*, interpersonal relationships, and especially the quality of the relationality within the living situation or congregation.

In time, religious moved to phase three, and turned from identity to *mission* statements. The concern here was with *service to others* outside the congregation. Diversity in ministry was by now an accepted fact, and decisions about apostolate were mutually discerned rather than unilaterally appointed. If unilateralness was operative, it was on the part of the individual religious, because at this point few superiors would dare. In fact, individual religious were often expected to find their own ministry. Living situations also became increasingly diverse. More and more individual religious and individual houses began making local decisions. And often these decisions were determined and influenced by the demands of ministry. In phase three, the emphasis was on *mission*, ministry, and service for others.

The overall movement in this second process of change suggests a move from a "herd" mentality to a "jungle" mentality with *individuality* at its peak. This movement toward individuality was much more than adaptation. If I can use as overriding labels *identity statement/search for intimacy/mission statement*, I would like to suggest viewing these three phases of this second level of change as that of *maturation*. For some time I have mused over the similarity between these three phases of change in religious life and Erik Erikson's fifth, sixth, and seventh stages of the life cycle: identity formation of adolescence, intimacy of young adulthood, and generativity, i.e. service and care of others in adulthood. I would contend that pre-Vatican II religious life, at least in the mid-twentieth century, was an archaic and childish way of life in which religious were passive, compliant, and dependent. And while the first process of ADAPTATION dealt with the archaic dimension, MATURATION into adulthood was necessary to deal with the childish dimension moving religious from passive/compliant/dependent children toward becoming active/dynamic/independent adults.

Evolution

At the same time we were *adapting* and *maturing*, another process of change was taking place. I suspect it is this third process of change that occasions some tension between U.S. religious and Rome. I would call this third process of change *evolution*.

First of all, it is probably somewhat erroneous to consider Vatican II the initial change agent in our lives. Vatican II happened because the Roman Catholic Church, like all people, groups, institutions, nations, and cultures—like all the world—is part of creation history and subject to the same evolutionary process that all creation and all history experiences. Surely Vatican II was a major transition point for the church. McBrien describes it as the movement from an enculturated western civilization Roman Catholic Church to a "world Church."[1] But the "global village" concept was already a well-used McLuhanism in the 1960s and described the changes recognized and occurring in the world society. That is, the church is part of the world—truly a graced and privileged part—but still a part, and therefore also part of God's evolutionary plan. Was it a coincidence that the upheaval of the 1960s in the U.S. and world society and the dramatic changes of Vatican II happened in the same decade? Was it a coincidence that as religious sought their identity, their roots, in their founders/foundresses, the miniseries *Roots*, which spoke of identity and rootedness, broke all records for TV-viewing audiences? The world, society, church, and religious are all on the same journey. And so women and men religious in the U.S., freed from an archaic lifestyle and maturing into more active/dynamic/independent adults, found themselves also in the midst of a major worldwide societal shift.

In Toffler's words, it is a shift from a "second wave" industrial civilization where nations competed for power and supremacy to a "third wave" technological civilization where every people, culture, and society share the same backyard. In reading Toffler's *Third Wave*, Naisbitt's *Megatrends*, Ferguson's *Aquarian Conspiracy*, or any of the other futurists, it became clear that the move from second wave to third wave is not just another generational move to bigger/faster/more. Industrialism was much more than an economic, social, political system. It was a way of life and a way of *thinking*. In fact, it was *primarily* a way of thinking. And the real change from second wave to third wave civilization is a change in thinking: in perceiving, understanding, conceptualizing.

The thinking of any civilization is affected by the imagery that explains and gives meaning and understanding to their experience. Primitive people explained natural phenomena as the work of the gods. The imagery of the world (world view) that was the controlling factor in the second wave/western industrialized civilization (1750–1950) was Newtonian science. For second wave people the entire universe was an understandable and predictable "machine," and everything from heavenly bodies to the smallest atom followed simple mathematically expressed rules and laws. It was a law-dominated image of the world. Buried within this "world view" was the implication that people and society, like atoms, behaved in the same way. Newton (1750) gave us the laws that governed atoms/heavens; Darwin (1882) gave us laws of social evolution; Freud (1900) gave us laws of the human psyche. People, like atoms, were considered "the same" and therefore interchangeable. In time Henry Ford came up with replaceable workers on the assembly line, congregations with replaceable religious in the classroom, and the church with replaceable priests in the parish. Second wave industrial, machine-like, law-determined thinking—while not the same as—was compatible with passive/compliant/dependent childish existence. Follow the rules and do as you are told.

Toffler insists that much of today's confusion is a cultural war between second wave and third wave thinking. Second wave thinking based on Newtonian science has been replaced by Einstein's *Theory of Relativity* (1905), Heisenberg's *Uncertainty Principle* (1931), Bertalanffy's *General Systems Theory* (1950). The result is that the second wave world view of reality—mechanistic, isolated atoms, predictable laws—gave way to a third wave view of reality—diversity, variables in relationship, open systems. And this play of diverse variables is no longer subject to predictable laws. Instead there are multiple options that govern our universe. It is no longer an either/or world, but a both/and world. The fact is that the "world view" *has* changed. And, as with previous world views, these scientific discoveries soon influenced our thinking about individuals, groups, and organizations. And so, religious clarifying their own identity—who I am/where I stand in relation to the world around me—had to do so at the same time the world view itself was changing.

The church as being part of the world was also affected by this change. *Gaudium et Spes* said, "The human race has passed from a static concept of reality to a more dynamic and evolutionary one."[2] And McBrien talks about the shift from pre- to post-Vatican II theology being due to a fundamental shift in methodology (thinking) from classicism to historical consciousness.[3]

Classicism is a "philosophical world view which holds that reality (truth) is essentially static, unchanging, and unaffected by history. Such truth can readily be captured in propositions or statements whose meaning is fixed and clear from century to century."[4] Historical consciousness "is a theological and philosophical mentality which is attentive to the impact of history on human thought and action, and which, therefore, takes into account the concrete and changeable."[5] According to McBrien, even into the 1950s the emphasis on moral theology was on the individual act (like the isolated atom) to determine whether or not it fell into the category of sin, and if so whether mortal or venial. "Stress was placed on obedience to the law: divine, natural, human. The 'good' is what is commanded by law. Therefore, *conformity to the law* is the fulfillment of the good."[6] It was simpler back then. There was little decision-making—just whether or not to follow the law. And in following the laws religious remained passive, compliant, and dependent. But Nuremberg, Mylai, Watergate made it increasingly clear that *compliance* to authority is not always moral. McBrien makes the distinction, "A moral theology founded on historical consciousness stresses personal (adult) responsibility: to God, to oneself, to the Church, and to the wider human community."[7] It does not reject the place of norms and obligations. But norms and obligations never adequately embody or capture the values they espouse. So while values may be absolute, the norms to realize the value are relative to the historical situation.[8] Prior to Vatican II, religious lived in a law-determined church and simply obeyed. Now religious had to evaluate the situation, interpret the norms, and make decisions. This *evolutionary* process, like the maturational process, brought religious to a position which required adult responsibility and necessitated on-going personal evaluation, interpretation and decision-making.

Transformation

Finally, a fourth process of change was operative in religious life following Vatican II. McEleny, commenting on *Perfectae Caritatis,* clarifies the distinction between "adaptations"—those changes necessary due to the contemporary needs of our time—and "renewal"—an interior renovation of the Spirit.[9] Without doubt this interior renovation has been a key characteristic of religious renewal in the United States. When speaking to the 1977 Inter-American Conference, Tillard said, "The main line of religious renewal in North America is a renewed emphasis on prayer and spiritual encounter with God."[10] Certainly spiritual direction, directed retreats, and the development of a personal prayer life increased the *individuality* and *diversity* of the God relationships of religious. Such spiritual development was increasingly compatible with the maturation of the individual and with the changes in theology. McBrien contrasts the regimented piety of the nineteenth century with that of the mid-twentieth saying, ". . . spiritualities began to emerge which are more world centered (Teilhard), neighbor-oriented (Van Zeller), justice concerned (Merton), and person integrating (Goldbruner) without prejudice at all to the traditional contemplative elements."[11] Such spiritual development was strongly incarnational, gospel-oriented, and social justice-minded.

This fourth process of change, *transformation*, is similar to, but not the same as, metanoia—conversion. It may be a third-wave way of thinking about spiritual development in contrast to a second wave. It is not a turning away from the "profane" world. Nor is it the identification and renunciation of that which is negative/unholy. Rather it is an increasingly in-depth transformation of self, group, the world at the heart of who we are, and of who God has created and calls us to be. The relevancy of this fourth process of change to our concern about religious life is that in developing a personal relationship with God, religious became aware of having their *own* eyes and ears of faith, their *own* gospel vision, the ability to see and hear God's call in a wide variety of places which *they* experienced. And so religious were no longer dependent on the "switchboard" approach to God's will through a superior. They could dial direct! And in that direct, unique, personal, Spirit-filled relationship there was often a passionate drivenness no superior could ever impel, a joyful spending of self no law or rule could ever demand, and at times there was a direction no constitution ever laid out. But God did not always go by the book. God asked a virgin to bear a child. This *transformation* process meant that religious had to listen and discern what the Spirit was saying to *them*. It was based on a deep personal relationship with God and added to the *individuality* seen in the maturation process of becoming active/dynamic/independent adults, and to the individual *responsibility* in the evolutionary process which requires personal evaluation, interpretation, and decision-making. And so all three processes seem to have brought religious to the same place: from being passive, compliant, dependent children who follow the rules/laws and accept God's will from superiors, to active, dynamic, independent adults who exercise responsible decision-making and mutually discern God's call.

Yet these three processes of increasing maturation, evolution, and transformation were necessary differentiations which only paved the way for additional development, for integration, for movement beyond active/dynamic/independent to interactive/resonant/interdependent. But religious cannot make that next move alone, independently. Religious came from pre-Vatican II, each on his or her own path. They had to. It was the only way to individuate. But the next move forward cannot be made without others—without authentic community. Community is not the living situation, not playing together, not dressing alike, not working in the same facility. Authentic community is the result of a bondedness around a common mission, Christ's mission, the kingdom, according to the spirit and charism of the founder/foundress as experienced by this particular group. And so religious need to work at bringing about authentic community within their congregations and wherever they minister, for in doing this they most truly carry out their mission, Christ's mission—that the kingdom will come.

Notes

1. Richard McBrien, *Catholicism* (Minneapolis: Winston Press, 1981), p. 607.

2. *Gaudium et Spes, The Pastoral Constitution on the Church in the Modern World*, n. 5. Cf. Walter Abbott, *The Documents of Vatican II* (New York: Guild Press, 1966), p. 204.

3. Richard McBrien, *Catholicism*, p. 941 (parenthetical remarks added).

4. Ibid., p. 1238.

5. Ibid., p. 1245.

6. Ibid., p. 936.

7. Ibid., p. 942 (parenthetical remark added).

8. Ibid.

9. Cf. Abbott, op. cit., pp. 464–465.

10. Jean Marie Tillard, "Religious Life Tomorrow," *Donum Dei* 24, *Canadian Religious Conference*, 1978, p. 149.

11. Richard McBrien, *Catholicism*, p. 1095.

The Profound Changes in
Religious Life Since Vatican II

Dianne Bergant, C.S.A.

It has become clear in the recent past that the ways in which we understood the world, society and human endeavor no longer seem adequate to meet and interpret the realities facing us. We should not then be surprised if we experience the same kind of disorientation in theology or in the religious practices of our faith.

World War II, with its Dresden and Auschwitz and Hiroshima, shattered the myth of the eschatological possibilities of godless progress. The world saw that technology could lead to its destruction just as well as it might lead to its perfection. It certainly could not return to a pre-scientific perspective, but neither had it devised an alternative way of understanding its achievements or its future. Recognizing this crisis within society, Pope John XXIII convoked Vatican II in order to bring the "vivifying and perennial energies of the gospel" to a world in desperate need of finding meaning and direction.

Pope John took a bold stand in suggesting that the church not only could address but even in some sense could meet the needs of the modern world, for as society was rushing into the scientific-technological age, in many ways the church was more and more entrenching itself in patterns of the past. This man was convinced of the compassionate love of God for all people, and he believed that the dynamic Spirit of God could and would refashion the church, making it a vibrant means of bringing God's love to the contemporary world.

The first item on his agenda was an updating of the church itself. All structures, patterns of behavior and attendant theological understandings were to be critiqued and, if need be, renewed. It soon became clear that updating might not be enough. Renewal would have to reach to the very roots of the church's reality. Thus, while the world was experiencing significant upheaval, the church deliberately entered into a more extensive self-overhauling in order to assist the world in its search for the future. It is within this context that the turbulence experienced within religious life must be seen if it is to be properly understood and addressed.

The Church in the Modern World

Pope John XXIII was not the only one to take a bold step. The participants of the council embodied this same boldness in issuing one, and only one, pastoral constitution, entitled *The Church in the Modern World*. It is, in fact, the only such document produced in the church's long history, and its very title alerts us to the extent of its departure from previous perceptions. This is not a dogmatic constitution intended to elicit adherence. It is a pastoral document meant to direct the church toward service in and to the contemporary world.

In compliance with this historic statement, the church has taken a daring stand. Without denying its responsibility of preserving the truth with which it has been entrusted, it now publicly assumes an attitude of humble service. Rather than calling for movement of the world to the church where salvation is found, the document calls for movement of the church into the world in order to transform it. Service to the world is a primary theme of the pastoral constitution.

A second point to be noted is that the council addressed the church's role in the *modern* world. Although acknowledging the fact that the contemporary world is not only secular but in many ways godless, the church does not reject this world but embraces it as one would embrace a loved one who has been blinded and lost. "God so loved the world . . ." The church is called to love the world in like manner and to bring the Christ of God into its midst.

The modern world is committed to search and research, to analysis and control. It is proud and materialistic and self-determined. If the church is to be the leaven of its transformation it must enter deeply into the concerns and the experience of this world. It cannot merely observe it from afar and prescribe treatment. The church commits itself to service and serious dialogue with this world, convinced that in the light of faith it can contribute toward a joint effort at greater understanding and transformation. The modern world makes tremendous demands upon itself. The church can expect nothing less if it immerses itself in this world.

Finally, being in the world as an agent of its transformation is quite different from withdrawing from it in order to be saved from its inherent evils. This shift in perspective suggests a significant change in soteriological understanding. In the past, withdrawal seemed necessary in order to be saved *from* the world. Now, involvement *in* the world is seen as contributing to the salvation *of* the world.

The contemporary church can no longer stand aloof from the struggling, faltering world as if secure in its possession of the means of salvation and willing to share them only with those who agree to conform to its pattern. This manner of being the presence of Christ in the world may have been effective at another time, but it would be counter-productive today. The church must attempt to do, with and for an otherwise efficient world, what this world cannot do by and for itself. Further, it must do it collaboratively in contemporary terms in the midst of the contemporary world.

Implications for Religious

These societal and ecclesial changes had profound repercussions in religious life. The collapse of both cultural and religious worldviews left many bereft of their sense of identity and their means of support. After having developed a defensive attitude toward the world with its values and projects and strategies, a world from which they had withdrawn, they were now expected to enter into and interact with this world, evaluate it according to criteria not fully developed, and lead it toward goals not yet clear. They were expected to relinquish a worldview which long had envisioned Christendom as the heart of civilization from which and to which flowed all divine grace. They were expected to espouse a worldview wherein the church was a collaborating agent for establishing the realm of God rather than the equivalent of it.

Individual religious and entire communities faced this transition with varying degrees of success and/or failure. The span of twenty years may be too short a time to have developed criteria for deciding just exactly what constitutes success or failure. However, the changes that have taken place can be examined against the ecclesial model set forth by the pastoral constitution. What follows is merely a summary of some of the obvious changes. (The order in which they appear is not intended as a prioritizing.)

Solidarity with the whole human family.

The first theme found in the preface to the pastoral constitution is solidarity with the human race and its history. In an attempt to be true to this ecclesial stance, religious have taken steps to relinquish their privileged status. They have tried to insert themselves into the mainstream of society by choosing to live closer to and more like others, becoming more self-determined and assuming more responsibility. Dress has been modified or drastically changed. Practices of silence have been dropped, as has a tightly regulated horarium. Life has moved from the confines of the convent into the world. It has become difficult to recognize a member of a religious community. Frequently the externals of identification are gone completely.

A lifestyle established over a hundred years or more, to which members had faithfully committed themselves, has been altered almost overnight, resulting in considerable pain and confusion for many members and sharp criticism from non-members. The extent to which individuals and communities experienced this differed both in expectation and in actual accomplishment. Hundreds have been disillusioned with this venture as variously realized in religious communities. This might explain why many of them departed. It is not only inaccurate but unfair to suggest that religious were just waiting for the chance to loosen up the constraints of their life. This may have been true for some, and the call to renewal may have provided these with the opportunity to leave with less opposition and shame, but most religious began to identify with the world primarily in response to the church's exhortation.

The real cause for alarm is not that religious have begun to identify with the world, but that in doing so some seem to have lost their religious identity. At times the renewal consisted of a superficial updating, i.e. the mere replacement of externals of lifestyle which had originated in a previous age. In some instances they did not first thoroughly examine their lifestyle in order to discover the underlying religious value that informed it and that might lend itself to contemporary expression. Here religious risked falling into a kind of accommodation to the world rather than undergoing authentic renewal. It gradually became clear that people with religious aspirations would neither choose to enter nor persevere in a community that was merely a caricature of what it claimed to be.

The myth that work is prayer developed on the heels of apostolic consciousness. The lines between ministerial activity and activism, which at best are blurred, at times seemed to disappear altogether, and people who had not yet developed the skills of discernment were often swept away with the currents of the time. Their willingness to be available was not always balanced, and energies of the community as well as of the individual were then strained. When left unattended, there resulted what has come to be known as "burn out."

Only genuine religious insight can perceive the transcendent dimension of reality. Good will does not guarantee the possession of this insight. When religious practices are merely set aside because they are judged irrelevant and their underlying religious value is not given new expression, people may venture into the world without a spirituality that can adequately sustain them. Apostolic religious may be convinced that the sacred cannot be sought apart from the world, but many still fail to discover its locus within the world. This may well be the most serious religious challenge facing them today and it certainly contributes to the decline in membership.

The signs of the times.

In the very first paragraphs of the pastoral constitution and throughout all of the major council documents, the church is directed to read the signs of the times, to discern them in the light of the gospel, and thus to be guided in its efforts to transform the world. Some of the issues the world faces include the inadequacy and injustice of the current patterns of growth and prosperity, the exploitation of natural resources, the population explosion, a world economy that seems out of control, disregard for environmental balance, and the tyranny of social systems that inhibit rather than promote well-being, to say nothing of the specter of nuclear confrontation. This is the world into which religious ventured. With the rest of the church, they were sent to address these urgent problems.

The painstaking study of the history of their community and of the character of their founding charism led religious to understand how their original ministries had addressed the societal needs of an earlier time. It challenged them to discover ways in which their present ministries might so function in a new era. This led to the revitalization and expansion of much of what they were doing. It also resulted in their handing some traditional ministries over to others within the church, and in their searching out new ways of establishing the realm of God.

Today religious are involved in advocacy programs, providing direct social service, influencing policy on all levels of government, working toward environmental control, promoting justice and peace in the world. Their involvement in these areas takes new forms. More frequently than not, they are working outside of traditional church structures and approved ministries. This is not because they have moved away from the work of the church, but because the official church has not yet moved to where they are ministering. They have done this, by and large, with the consent and support of their respective communities and, therefore, consider themselves obedient to the call of the church through their own religious superiors.

Religious encountered obstacles and experienced tension and ambiguity as they embarked on new paths of ministry. The particular level of competence that they had achieved in their traditional ministries was not always achieved in their new work. They quickly realized that high ideals and good will are soon exhausted if they are not accompanied by specialized preparation and an acquaintance with the dynamics operative in the respective field. It was not uncommon that religious experienced failure in their early attempts at service and their spirits were, in some instances, broken in the process.

For others the situation was quite the opposite. They were not only equal to the task at hand, but they and their ministry flourished. The opposition they faced came from unexpected quarters. The very church they believed had commissioned them seemed unconcerned with, even resistant to, their work. It appeared to many that maintaining the status quo was preferred to evangelization and that outdated ecclesiastical structures were preferred to the dynamic Spirit of God. Many of these religious lost confidence in the church and some left their congregations.

In many ways religious are on the cutting edge of the church's ministry. They are active in new frontiers where the terrain is unfamiliar and there are few guidelines to follow. However, belonging to a religious community makes them in some way public witnesses to ecclesial involvement. The connection between religious initiative in ministry and ecclesiastical approval is fraught with difficulties today. In some instances the tension had reached crisis proportions. Today membership in a religious community demands that one be willing to enter into the struggle and there work with all parties toward a resolution.

A lay-centered church.

The major documents of Vatican II all stress the dignity and responsibility of *all* the people of God. The church is no longer to be identified with the hierarchy. The sacraments of initiation open the doors to an active role in the mission of the church to transform the world. Many of the laity have taken their call quite seriously and have been directly or indirectly involved in both traditional and non-traditional ministries. They are frequently found side by side with religious, assuming the same responsibilities and sharing the same satisfaction and disappointment. There may have been a time when layfolk were considered substitutes for absent religious. That time is long past. They are now ministers in their own right and by their own choice, and they are as committed and as professionally prepared as are their religious counterparts.

This means that today there are many options available to those interested in ministry. It is no longer necessary to join a religious community in order to serve within the church. One need not be a male celibate cleric to have religious influence. There are many opportunities for women or men, married or single or religious, in traditional or non-traditional service, for a period of time or for a lifetime. This situation has significantly influenced the size of religious communities.

Challenge for the Future

The twenty years since the close of Vatican II have brought profound changes in religious life. Some of these changes have been simple adaptation to the contemporary world. Others have resulted from the probing of religious institutions and practices in order to discover their underlying traditional religious value, the first step of the hermeneutical process analyzed earlier. It is safe to say that religious have been addressing the other points of the process as well, i.e. searching for ways of discerning the *real* religious needs of the moment and bringing traditional religious values to bear on these needs. It is not enough to approach these tasks with faith and commitment. Serious examination, rigorous evaluation, and faithful reinterpretation are required and this approach calls for extensive knowledge, keen insight and creative imagination. Perhaps the most demanding aspect of this entire enterprise is the task of deciding upon the appropriate criteria for analysis and evaluation at each step in the process.

Like our predecessors in past periods of crisis, in many

ways we are in uncharted waters. Therefore, we must be steadfast without being unyielding, bold without being foolhardy, confident without being presumptuous, creative without being forgetful. In all of this we must be humble as together we search for ways to respond to God.

A More Limited Witness:

An Historical Theologian Looks at the Signposts

Mary Ann Donovan, S.C.

Something new is appearing in the American church. That new thing is a more limited witness that has a specific emphasis on the practice of celibacy for the sake of the kingdom. There are a number of signposts that point this way. Prominent ones are posted by society, by the church and the situation of women religious within the church, and by the situation of the potential candidates. I will first try to decipher some of these signposts. Then I will describe what I think is the general nature of our journey.

Some time ago I invited women and men in various parts of the country to join in my reflection on factors that influence the decision to enter religious life today. I have quoted some of their remarks in what follows.

Societal Factors Affecting the Entry Rate

Let us grant that culture opposes the values that religious life stands for. This has consistently been the case in the history of religious life and is not new. I wish rather to isolate three other societal factors which appear to affect choice today. The nuclear issue is critical. Reflective young adults ask: "Is there to be a normal lifetime?" "Can I expect to live out the decade?" Evidently for some the response to the threat of nuclear catastrophe is a form of paralysis. It becomes impossi-

84

ble to plan a life choice or to decide a life work. A Vietnam veteran in his mid-thirties explains: "It's impossible to think of a normal lifetime. It's too long. A year is O.K.; five years is a stretch. I can't see beyond that." Yet some are impelled by similar considerations to enter religious life. Their perspective on the choice is provocative. A novice in her mid-twenties maintains: "The only possible commitment is to peace. Anything else has to come step by step. I can commit to the novitiate, then to the next stage. I can't think farther." A society on the brink of self-destruction offers its younger members little scope and less motivation for long-range planning. How can religious communities respond to such a dilemma? Possibly the only useful response is dedication to the cause of peace and nuclear disarmament. The American bishops indicated as much in outlining the elements of a pastoral response to the dilemma of our time.

A second societal factor related to the nuclear issue, but also found independently of reflection on that issue, is the difficulty with permanent commitment. Process and change are values in themselves in our country today. We see this in a marketplace geared to disposability and replacement, in the expectation that occupational mobility is desirable, in the expectation that moving from house to house, from county to county, even from state to state is normal, and in the rapidly escalating divorce rate with the accompanying reconstitution of families. In this situation merely to contemplate a permanent relationship to a religious congregation is in itself already a counter-cultural stance. By contrast, limited commitment is attractive. What are the implications of the flood of applications for the Jesuit International Volunteers? In the spring of 1985 there were 85 complete applications for 22 places; the 22 accepted completed training and are now in service. At the national level there are as of this writing 313 Jesuit Volunteers. The southwest story is typical: 110 applied for 62 places. At a minimum, this reflects the willingness of young people to engage in direct, *short term* service. ROTC enlistment is a related phenomenon, and quite consistent with one interpretation of the nuclear issue. It has the added benefit of offering both educational and job training at a time when the young person needs both in the struggle toward self-identity. Congregations and dioceses need to consider a variety of ways to make available a temporary relationship.

A third societal factor is the gains for women won through the feminist movement. As women attain more equal education and as opportunities for achievement within the society open, however slowly, one attraction of religious life is removed. Religious life has made available careers and leadership opportunities otherwise not open to women. The life may not have been consciously chosen for these reasons, but that the life offered opportunities once not available elsewhere remains a fact. This pattern of particular opportunities available only through the religious life replicates on a smaller scale what is true on a larger scale of the life itself. In its origins and throughout its history, religious life has functioned as *the* alternative to marriage for Roman Catholic women. I will turn briefly to that history.

Examination of the apocryphal writings of the second and third centuries (a body of the popular literature of the day) makes clear that the development of the choice of a life of religiously dedicated chastity was viewed as the development of a life option for women opposed to the socially approved pattern of marriage.[3] Since the institutionalization of the monastic life in the late fourth century, the options available to women in the west have been marriage or religious life. The monastic life itself was increasingly a cloistered life for women from the sixth century.[4] Despite the efforts of lay women like the beguines, of the mendicant third orders, and of women concerned to live an apostolic life—women like Angela de

Merici and Mary Ward—the cloister or marriage remained the available options until the work of Vincent de Paul and Louise de Marillac in the seventeenth century. With their break-through, the options became cloister, service in the convent, or marriage. Even here, church legislation did not recognize women with simple vows as "religious" until 1900. At that time the impact of the work of women like Catherine McAuley was indirectly recognized.[5] Thus the cloister, the convent, and marriage remained the primary options for women until the last twenty-five years. With the opening of other opportunities to women, religious life has become less attractive.

Factors Situated within the Church

Religious life might not have become less attractive if it were not for a number of additional factors which are immediately situated within the church itself. I wish to single out three of these factors which I identify as *the emerging lay role, the institutional face of the church,* and *the current situation of women religious in the church.*

The emerging lay role. Here I am using terms "lay" and "laity" to denote those members of the church who are neither clerics nor bound by public religious profession.[6] It is a common conviction that *the* crisis today is not one of religious vocations but rather one of the emergence of the lay vocation within the church. This has been shaped by the Vatican II decree on the laity, as well as by both the content and placing of the chapters on the laity and on the call of the whole church to holiness in the council's dogmatic constitution on the Church. This conciliar emphasis is but the next development in a series easily traceable from the nineteenth century here and in Europe: the impact of papal teaching on social justice, the Knights of Labor in late nineteenth century America, fraternal organizations like the Knights of Columbus, the retreat movement, the Christian Family Life movement, the Catholic Action movement of the 1930s and 1940s, and the liturgical movement (oriented toward development of the lay apostolate from the 1930s to the 1950s). Now, in the 1970s and 1980s we are seeing laity take their place in catechesis, liturgical life, and the service ministries. Roles they fill are roles that religious and, in some cases, priests used to fill. After all, the call to minister in the church flows neither from religious profession nor from ordination but is part of the common call to discipleship and flows from baptism. The shift is in *who* ministers. The same ministries are being performed. Now it is often a lay woman or a lay man who performs them. This is entirely right and proper. In fact, one role for religious in the current situation is to facilitate this development. As one brother put it: "We must decrease to permit them to increase. In relation to this development we will be and look different." The emerging lay role is a positive development within the church which has consequences for the phenomenon of religious life.

The institutional face of the church. Lay leaders share with the religious the encounter with the institutional face of the church. The face which the institutional church turns toward church members, as well as toward non-members, is a face whose lineaments are often hardened by clericalism and by the accompanying patriarchalism which is destructive of healthy relationships among adults, and in particular between women and men. My understanding of these two phenomena is that presented in the Conference of Major Superiors of Men's 1983 study. There clericalism is identified as:

> . . . the conscious or unconscious concern to pro-
> mote the particular interests of the clergy and to
> protect the privileges and power that have tradition-
> ally been conceded to those in the clerical state. . . .

Among its chief manifestations are an authoritarian style of ministerial leadership, a rigidly hierarchical world view, and a virtual identification of the holiness and grace of the church with the clerical state and, thereby, with the cleric himself.[7]

This attitude is rooted in the social reality of patriarchal culture which:

. . . is characterized by several features: the institutionalization of male privilege and power and an accompanying social mythology to account for it, the social and cultural inequality of men and women and the assumption that this represents the appropriate (even God-given) pattern for all social relationships, and the formation and legitimation of vertical structures of power that are based on the presumed superiority and inferiority of given classes of people.[8]

The document points out that clericalism has clear connections with patriarchal culture in its assumptions about social structures, the vertical lines of authority and power, and the privileges of caste. Such a situation is destructive of the emergence of lay roles in the church. It is particularly harmful to women in that it reinforces a subordinate and passive role for women. The perception of the institutional church as clerical and patriarchal, and so as male biased and female exploitative, is a serious impediment facing gifted and independent women considering a vocation to religious life in the church.

The current situation of women religious in the church. As if the perception of the institutional church as clerical and patriarchal weren't enough to give a thoughtful woman pause, unfortunately to that image must be added the present situation of women's religious congregations vis-à-vis the institutional church. Here again there are three neuralgic areas: the process for approval of the constitutions of congregations, the handling of cases like those of the signers of the *New York Times* ad, and the papal intervention in apostolic religious life in the United States. In terms of the process for approval of constitutions, it is apparent to the thoughtful potential candidate that women have struggled for some years, at the behest of the Holy See,[9] to renew their congregations in an appropriate manner. The process for approval of constitutions is experienced as often arbitrary, sometimes uninformed, and lacking in sensitivity to the particularly feminine embodiment of religious life emerging in the newly developed structures.[10] At this level all elements of collegiality appear often to be lost in a call for a kind of submission which reflects the worst elements of the clerical and patriarchal system. Ought not a woman to question whether she should spend her life engaging in such a system? Do we not come to religious life to live out the charism of our congregation within the family of the church, rather than to live out a univocal charism of religious life controlled by the authority of the ecclesial institution? Women—both potential candidates and seasoned religious—have difficulty here.

A similar difficulty centers around the handling of the signers of the *New York Times* ad. My concern here is not with the details of the case, but with how church authorities handled it. The action involved judgment without inquiry; indeed it was immediate, arbitrary, and heavily authoritarian. Again, what is perceived and experienced are the worst aspects of clericalism and patriarchalism. Ought not a woman to question whether she should entrust her life to a system whose workings are marked not by mutual respect and trust, but by the heavy-handed exercise of power? Do we not come to religious life to serve one another as disciples of Jesus, out of love for him present in his body the church? Women suffer painfully when that very body turns against them in an arbitrary way, without respect for them and their congregations.

The papal intervention in American apostolic religious life at first engendered fear analogous to that experienced in the aftermath of the case just mentioned. The problem here again was the apparent lack of trust on the part of the institutional church for American women religious. Through the instrumentality of the papal commission, that situation has developed into a potentially supportive and presently encouraging dialogue. Whether it is perceived as such or not by potential candidates remains a question. Women religious in this country are in a time of transition. For fifteen to twenty years sisters have been engaged in wholehearted efforts of renewal. What is needed is time to complete the process and then to appropriate what has been done. During this period the structures of the church can best assist by offering support, questioning, and encouragement. The pontifical commission has structured an intra-diocesan and intra-parish process which can enable the education of laity, priests, and bishops. As the dialogue continues it may encourage the consideration of religious vocation on the part of women and support of that vocation by family, friends, and interested clergy.

This brings me to the internal situation of women's religious congregations. When the potential candidate considers the congregations, what does she see? As one young woman put it, "If the members do not look convincing and convinced, forget it." Here there is a double problem. On the one hand, the problems connected with what I have called "the institutional face of the church" have in some cases engendered a climate in which it is very difficult to invite another woman in, to be properly welcoming to potential members. Families do not welcome guests during times of internal crisis, nor do they feel at ease welcoming the prospective spouses of their members at such times. So, too, it has been difficult for many religious women to encourage candidates when they themselves feel somewhat "under siege." Likewise, the very tenuousness of a time of transition does not create a good climate for the induction of new members. On the other hand, a second problem is connected directly with the declining numbers. There is an element here of self-fulfilling prophecy. The religious who dwells on the few numbers invites few in and so her congregation has yet fewer numbers. Whether we look at the problems connected with the institutional face of the church and the transition stage of religious congregations, or at the problems connected with shrinking numbers, we are dealing with a matter of morale and the ability of group members to generate new membership. The Spirit has always worked through the internalized living out of the charism of the group, a living out characterized by joy, to draw new members to congregations. Where that is not present, it is not surprising that new members do not come.[11]

Yet there are other questions we religious women must ask ourselves when we contemplate our declining numbers. Are we counter-cultural enough? Are we *perceived* as giving of ourselves, our very selves? Is our identity evident to the average Catholic today? What of the struggle to live simply that others may simply live, while at the same time operating at levels of professional excellence to serve in the apostolate? This needs to be communicated. The amount of salary given to the common fund, the embracing of simple living in the face of materialism and even opulence, the willing dedication to celibate loving in the face of a sexually permissive culture, the discipline of self-will in the face of a me-first culture—this struggle to live the gospel needs to be communicated. We need, too, to communicate the nature of our faith commitment, that deepest part of our lives. Our professionalism is apparent; what about what is in our hearts? Most of us are quite protective about that. We need, finally, to communicate our new-found sense of the community that exists in the midst of diverse lifestyles. We are learning to nurture the bond that unites us in many ways other than common roof and table. Have we made this apparent? One mother comments: "Unless you have a strong sense of community, what is there that my daughter can find among you that she cannot find as a single lay worker in the church?" Here the continuation of the dialogue process initiated by the pontifical commission is critical. We have dialogued at length (some would say ad nauseum!) with one another about our changing understanding of religious life. We need to invite clergy and laity into the conversation, both to communicate what we have learned, and to learn from them as we struggle with the problems that are still with us. Not the least of these problems are those that are due to the uneven pace at which members assimilate renewal, and their disagreements about its direction. Yet honest and open dialogue about our situation is a vital step in the nurturing of new vocations. With so few of us in the schools we must turn to new sources for contacts. An informed laity and clergy is a first step. A second involves our learning how to draw from those among whom and with whom we now work. This requires the sensitivity and patience to spend the time to nurture adult vocations which formerly was spent nurturing adolescent vocations.

Factors Concerning Potential Candidates

I turn now to the situation of potential candidates. There are a number of factors that we need to consider in contemplating the low entry rate. I referred previously to the nurturing of adult vocations, not adolescent vocations. One observation of those who are engaged in formation work is that the psychological maturing process is slower than the physical maturation. That phenomenon is not restricted to persons presently in the formation process. The lengthy time spent in education, with the correlative delay of entry into adult life projects, has implications for readiness to make life choices. The situation is not simply that religious are no longer in schools in large numbers; it is also that students in schools are less ready to make life choices. Their interest in religion is high but it seems to be paired with low interest in institutional forms of religious commitment.

We also need to know why the poor—and particularly ethnic groups—have had difficulty both entering and remaining in congregations. Here we need to examine our own prejudices, as well as the cultures of the ethnic groups which form an increasingly large segment of American Catholics.

With the older and more mature candidate, there is the question of how we incorporate members already established in careers. With the younger candidate we must recognize the problem for a young person entering an older group: Does the woman of twenty-five or twenty-six want to accept responsibility for a future with women whose median age is between fifty-five and sixty-five? Is she willing to do this without a strong peer group?

Thus, lack of readiness to make a life choice, lack of ability to attract and to retain the poor and ethnics, uncertainty about how to incorporate mature applicants, and the burdens assumed by the few young in a predominantly older group all are factors affecting recruitment rate. There are steps that can be taken to redress a number of these difficulties. Whether doing so will prove to be the long-term remedy is another question.

The Key Charism That Marks the Religious Life

What is most proper to religious life is the public profession of evangelical counsels by public vows. Those vows, and in particular the vow of celibacy for the sake of the kingdom, are absolutely distinctive of religious life. I would go so far as to name consecrated celibacy the ultimate, irreducible charism of religious life. To pledge celibacy for the kingdom is at the heart of religious life. To pledge celibacy for the kingdom constitutes the religious. All else follows on this.[13] It is not surprising that this insight should come to the fore in our sexually preoccupied culture.

Poverty marked the new age of religious life in the thirteenth century, a century of burgeoning wealth. A high regard for poverty marked the mendicant orders founded then.

Obedience characterized the new dawn of religious life in the late sixteenth and early seventeenth centuries. That time was coincident with the rise of individualism in its various manifestations. The Jesuits are an example of an order founded then which values obedience highly.

Sexuality is in many ways a dominant concern of much of our present-day society. The gift that witnesses to the transcendence of the gospel in the face of this preoccupation is consecrated celibacy. It is this vow taken for the sake of the kingdom which especially characterizes the witness of religious in American society.

How does this relate to the question of declining numbers of religious in the changed and changing situation of the church in the United States? I respond with another question: Does the prospective candidate enter in order to maintain a particular form of life, or to engage in witness with her sisters? The religious life does not exist for the apostolate and ought not to be identified with or reduced to its works. As it becomes clearer that there are not the numbers of religious required to maintain given works, it also becomes clearer that works are not (and never were) *the* key factor which identifies the religious. John Paul II reminds us of a long-standing tradition when he strongly situates religious vocation within the Christian vocation. He develops his understanding within the context of response to

95

the questions of "why be a human person" and "how." He remarks that religious vocation involves learning who one is in the act of a particular way of following Jesus.[14]

Our way of following Jesus is witness to the gospel through the public profession of the evangelical counsels, and most particularly through the public profession of celibacy for the sake of the kingdom. The life of consecrated celibacy will be filtered through the charism of the particular congregation, and so lived in varying circumstances, but it is recognizably a similar witness to the gospel in all the congregations. Following the Dominican tradition, Thomas Aquinas places the three vows as central and as principles. The ways in which one "disposes oneself to the observance of each" vary, and so orders vary from one another.[15] He finds room for works as widely varied as soldiering (he lived during the heyday of the military orders), business administration, and manual labor. His point is that anything can be done that helps our neighbor and serves God; it is the intent that matters.[16]

Religious today apply a similar principle in the attempt to relate the goals of foundresses and founders to changed circumstances. The combination of changed circumstances with declining numbers has led to dropped works. Is this in itself a sign of the decline of religious life? I think not. I listen again to Thomas, who reminds us that "the religious state is directed to the attainment of the perfection of charity, consisting principally in the love of God and secondarily in the love of neighbor. Consequently *that which religious intend chiefly and for its own sake is to give themselves to God*. Yet if their neighbor be in need, they should attend to his affairs out of charity. . . ."[17]

With his usual clarity Thomas subordinates works to the primary end of the life. That end was then and remains now the gift of self which constitutes a particular witness to the gospel. A key element of that witness is consecrated celibacy.

Today in our country that witness is vitally needed. Yet

celibacy is not the path for the many but for the few. The very nature of the kind of witness that is needed assures that numbers will remain small. As we gain clarity in this area, and sureness in living a life renewed in the spirit of our foundresses and founders and of the gospel, the candidates the Lord sends us will come. I think this will continue to be in small numbers. Our task is to enable the laity to assume their rightful role in the church and to be content with our smaller numbers. It is my conviction that a reduction in numbers does not constitute a crisis of vocations, but rather is God's unique gift to the American church today. Our journey today is a pilgrimage, one we make with our sisters and brothers, lay and cleric. Our role on the pilgrimage is to witness to the kingdom through lives of consecrated celibacy.

Notes

1. National Conference of Catholic Bishops, *The Challenge of Peace: God's Promise and Our Response* (USCC, 1983), #279–300.

2. For the changing status of women see Ruth Leger Sivari, *Women . . . A World Survey* (World Priorities, Box 25140: Washington, D.C., 1985); Maria Riley, "Women Are the Poor," *Center Focus* 63 (1984), p. 3; "Women in the U.S.—A New Look," *U.S. News and World Report* 93 (1982), pp. 54–55.

3. The evidence was studied by Virginia Burrus, *Chastity as Autonomy: Women in the Stories of the Apocryphal Acts, Studies in Women and Religion* 23 (Lewiston: Edwin Mellen, 1987).

4. On cloister of women religious see E. Jombart and M. Viller, "Clôture," *Dictionnaire de spiritualité* II.1, parts III–IV, cc. 987–1005.

5. "Conditae a Christo," Dec. 8, 1900, clarified the sta-

tus of religious with simple vows. Such congregations of either sex are identified as religious in the 1917 Code, canon 488. Their status remains unchanged by the present universal law.

6. While this usage does not correspond to canon 207 of the universal law, it is helpful for the present discussion.

7. CMSM Documentation, #37, April 8, 1983, p. 2.

8. Ibid., p. 8; see also p. 11.

9. See *Evangelica Testificatio*, #51–54.

10. See John M. Lozano, "Trends in Religious Life Today," *Review for Religious* 42 (1983), pp. 481–505, especially pp. 487–489.

11. See *Evangelica Testificatio*, #55.

12. Michael J. Buckley, "Reflections on the Document, 'Essential Elements,' " p. 269, in Robert J. Daly, et al., ed. *Religious Life in the U.S. Church: The New Dialogue* (Paulist: New York, 1984).

13. John M. Lozano develops a perspective similar to mine in *Discipleship: Towards an Understanding of Religious Life* (Claret: Chicago, 1983), pp. 122–128.

14. See *Redemptionis Donum*, #4–5; a parallel position is presented in "Essential Elements," #32–33.

15. *Summa Theologiae* II–II, q. 188, a. 1, ad 2.

16. See ibid., II–II, q. 188, a. 3, body.

17. Ibid., II–II, q. 187, a. 3, body.

Vanishing Church Professionals*

Joseph H. Fichter, S.J.

The precipitous decline in the number of Catholic seminarians and priests, and of women and men in religious communities, is a puzzling paradox at a time when divinity schools of certain conservative churches are overcrowded with ministerial candidates and when some Protestant denominations are actually faced with a clergy "oversupply."[1] Even during that triumphal period when the Catholic Church had the highest number ever of priests, sisters and brothers, some church officials were already concerned about the vocation "shortage."

Since the Second Vatican Council an almost endless series of conferences, symposia, lectures, articles, and books have dealt with the problem of ecclesiastical resignation. Most of these, however, were conducted or written by the people in charge—those organizationally responsible for governing church personnel. Recently there have been a number of explanations and descriptions coming from the resignees themselves. It is mainly to these "inside sources" that I have turned to seek explanations for the unprecedented large exodus of priests, sisters, and brothers. As Robert Merton[2] has noted, often the most significant insights can be gained from the outsiders who were once insiders.

*This is a condensation of Father Fichter's original article, "Vanishing Church Professionals," which appears as a chapter in the author's book, *The Sociologist Looks at Religion* (Michael Glazier, 1988). It appears here through the permission of the publisher.

What's Wrong with Leaving?

The church vocation has long been considered a strong moral commitment from which a person has no right to resign. The most permanent type of dedication was expected from those who were sacramentally ordained, and from the religious women and men who had pronounced solemn perpetual vows of obedience, chastity, and poverty. Everett Hughes spoke of the church vocation as the most enduring of all professions. Hughes noted that the person who leaves any profession "makes light of dedication to it, and calls upon himself that anger which reaches its extreme in the attitude toward a priest who gives up the cloth."[3] (A few years before his death in 1983 Professor Hughes did acknowledge that "things have changed.")

Traditionally it was felt that there was something "wrong" with a person's resignation from the life of religious consecration. Some people still are uneasy about consorting with an ex-priest, or even mentioning him, even when a legal dispensation has been granted by the Vatican. The mother of a former priest tells of her experience at morning mass in her parish church: "When my son was still a priest, the ladies were all smiles. They treated me like a special person. After he quit they avoided me. . . . They were embarrassed as though this were a family scandal you should try to hide." The American bishops' pastoral letter in 1968 said that Christian people are "scandalized by the derelict priest," and that even the sophisticated world itself takes scandal.

The "reasons" for which dispensations were granted during the process of laicization usually centered on what was seen as the moral failure of the person seeking the dispensation. The only "guiltless" situation was the rare case in which the sacerdotal ordination was found to have been invalid. And even then the terminology called the procedure a "dismissal," suggesting that it could not be an honorable and voluntary resignation. In most cases the individual had to admit some inadequacy or moral fault, usually a lack of steadfast virtue and inability to live a celibate life. There was never official recognition that others, such as an arrogant bishop or intolerant superior, might be at fault.

In one of my earlier studies of priestly defections I included an item in a questionnaire to priests, asking their opinion of the reason why priests leave. Practically all of the answers suggested failure on the part of the individual, usually centering around the theme of Punch and Judy or, as some said, "booze and babes." I wrote then that church officials and religious superiors usually interpreted this as "a personal breakdown of spiritual habits and values. The notion here is that the individual has become spiritually tepid through his own fault. He loses interest in prayer and meditation, neglects the rules and customs that are meant for his protection, becomes bored with the whole routine of the spiritual life."[4]

As for the matter of nuns' resignations, superioresses in several instances admitted no other reason than the fault of the subject. A typical response: "When nuns in perpetual vows forsake their vocation they are yielding to pride or an evil desire of the world." Another superioress said that "among the rare cases where nuns leave after perpetual vows, I note as causes mental instability and inconstancy, faults of character which, in spite of all hopes, prove impossible to correct, lack of affective attachment, and infidelity to prayer." Another comment: Sometimes the individual becomes restless and dissatisfied with convent life. There is a certain "hardening of the character which comes with increasing age. Sufficient fight has not been put up against defects which now become more apparent. They are inveterate habits that are impossible to get rid of now that moral strength is weakening along with physical."[5]

Absence of Vocation

The purpose of the novitiate training in religious orders, and of the seminary for diocesan priests, is to test whether the candidate actually has a vocation. There was a time when a large number of young Catholics were willing to "try out" their calling: they became ex-novices or ex-seminarians simply on the understanding that such was not their calling. As perceived by administrators in 1966, forty-seven percent of the sisters who left the religious life before last vows did so because they had "no vocation." This rose to sixty-five percent in 1982. "Psychological disturbance," given as a reason for forty-one percent of those who left in 1966, declined to eight percent in 1982.[6]

Aside from the inner urge and subjective attraction to full-time service of God and the church, there are no specific measurable criteria that guarantee the possession of a vocation. Certain personal qualities are expected, such as good health, general maturity, cooperative attitude, goodness of life, and sufficient intelligence. But, for priests, the authenticity of the vocation is canonically assured only when the man is accepted by the bishop for sacerdotal ordination; for religious, it is only when the superior of a religious congregation accepts the solemn vows of the candidate. Objectively, then, in accordance with canon law it is ordination or the official acceptance of the vows that guarantees the validity of the vocation.

Like baptism, the sacrament of holy orders is said to be indelible, and Vatican authorities are much more reluctant to grant dispensations to priests than to religious sisters and brothers. Even when a priest has been formally laicized, he may be reminded of the scriptural dictum, "Thou art a priest forever" (Ps 110).

The case is somewhat different for religious women who request a dispensation. One who left the sisterhood for "personal reasons" she refuses to discuss recalls the remarks of another former sister: "I always wanted to leave, but we were brainwashed in the idea that God wants me here. I felt constantly guilty because I was not happy. I probably never had a vocation. In fact, my vows probably weren't even valid." Another ex-nun remarked: "I never should have entered. It took me twenty years to realize that. I never was happy, and finally I got a sickness brought about by tensions and stress, and my psychiatrist showed me I had to get out."[7]

Monica Baldwin wrote a best-seller that described "the religious vocation from the point of view of one who had no such vocation." After ten years in the convent, she began to wonder whether she had made a "dreadful and tragic mistake." And after twenty-eight years as a contemplative nun, she knew that she "could blink the truth no longer. I was no more fitted to be a nun than to be an acrobat."[8]

It is not uncommon for an ex-sister or ex-priest to say that "I lost my vocation." The person of deep faith may suggest that God calls some people on a temporary rather than on a permanent basis. In most religious communities of brothers and sisters, vows are pronounced for a three year period. This is considered a kind of try-out, from which the individual is honorably released if so desired. The Daughters of Charity of St. Vincent de Paul have never taken perpetual vows and have remained uncloistered. They are not canonically defined as a religious congregation but are members of a "society of common life." The sister who declines to renew her vows may be said to have "lost" her vocation, or simply never to have had one.

Change of Commitment

In a survey of diocesan clergy, immediately after the Second Vatican Council, we found that almost two-thirds of the respondents (63.8%) agreed with the statement that "the church should allow voluntary resignation, or honorable discharge, from the priesthood."[9] The large proportion of priests who approved this notion was a genuine breakthrough, a first American indication that the permanency of priesthood could be seriously questioned. Even under conditions of an honorable discharge, however, the individual may claim that he is "not really leaving" the vocation of doing God's work on earth. One departing priest wrote to his friends and relatives that "I can better contribute to the work of bringing the good news of Christ to the world as a layman rather than as a member of the clergy. I still feel very deeply the call of the Spirit that brought me to ordination, but I can no longer correlate that call with my life as a member of the clergy."[10]

The one characteristic of the ecclesiastical vocation that distinguishes it from all other professional organizational situations is the individual's spiritual relationship with God. This unique characteristic, however, may suffer severe strain unless it exists within a supportive structural environment.

In their study of diocesan priests, Hall and Schneider[11] described the kind of organization to which individuals are likely to have a deep commitment. The first characteristic was the requirement for a long period of training to develop effective workers. The second characteristic was that stages of advancement through the seminary, and stages of promotion in the work career, occurred within the system; there was no lateral entry of "employees" from outside. Third, the work experience itself was deemed more important to effectiveness than the introduction of new technology. Fourth, the lifestyle of the employees was closely bound to their required professional functions. The clergy's home life was literally inseparable from their work life.

One may hypothesize that the quality of the individual's commitment will change to the extent that these four institutional characteristics change. It is evident that seminary training has been reconstituted and shortened. More priests now earn graduate degrees from outside educational institutions, and obtain promotions in church positions that require specialized technical knowledge. The importance and value of the celibate lifestyle is coming more and more into question. It is to be expected that role commitment will become more flexible under changing institutional circumstances. This may be interpreted as the price to pay for the aggiornamento of the Second Vatican Council. Adaptations in one part of the church are logically accompanied by changes in other areas of the church.

Mismanagement

There has been a singular lack of humility among church officials at both the local and the international levels in admitting that both poor performance by their subordinates, and their resignations, may often be ascribed to inept administration. Our earlier surveys of diocesan clergy have shown that clergy satisfaction and commitment is highest in those dioceses where the bishop demonstrates personal interest in the priests and where communications are good with the chancery officials. It is no secret that inadequate performance of roles may occur among persons in authority as well as among subordinates.

It appears that Pope Pius XII was aware of this organizational problem as early as 1951, when he called for adaptation of the customs and structures of religious communities. His advice to religious superiors could just as well have been addressed to diocesan officials and bishops.

Tension and resentment seem to be growing among American sisters over "vacillating" instructions from Rome. Paul VI mandated renewal in all religious communities. John Paul II ordered a reversal. Religious were informed in the 1983 document from the Sacred Congregation of Religious and Secular Institutes, *Essential Elements in the Church's Teaching on Religious Life*, that "the lessons learned from their two-decade experience of renewal are abrogated in favor of a return to a preconciliar closed system of religious life."[12] Even the sister superiors of religious communities were rankled by the arbitrariness of the peremptory order from Rome requiring sisters who signed the "Abortion Statement" in the *New York Times* advertisement a few years ago either to recant or be dismissed.

Many instances of mishandling, or poor human relations, are cited by men who have left the priesthood. One member of a missionary society recalled his swift removal from a diocese in the late 1960s. "Without giving me an interview, without personally phoning or writing me, I was notified by the pastor," he says. "There was no interview, no court of appeals, no review board."[13]

In the American bishops' study of resigned priests, three out of ten said that a "particular act of injustice by the superior" was crucial in influencing their decision to leave.[14] One of the most significant findings of that survey was the importance of abuses of authority in the minds of the priests surveyed. When asked to indicate a great personal problem to them in their priesthood, the largest proportion of respondents in every age category mentioned "the way authority is exercised in the church." Abuse of authority was the Number 1 complaint of fifteen personal problems of the clergy. Celibacy, incidentally, ranked fifth. And even for those who continue in the service of the church, the biggest source of bitterness and misery is the way authority is sometimes exercised.

Role Conflict

In the monastic tradition of the church, the tasks performed by monks and nuns were secondary to the central function of prayer and contemplation. It was said that "work is a form of prayer," *laborare est orare*, but in general the order of the day was so arranged that work was not allowed to interfere with prayer.

When work became a type of professional service to others, however, especially in schools and hospitals, this was not always possible. The question then arose as to whether one might conscientiously "break the rule" in order to attend to the demands of work. Today more and more clergymen feel that they are wearing two hats. There has been much misunderstanding about the dilemma of the hyphenated clergy, such as the priest-teacher or the priest-scientist. If the diocese or religious order is structured to allow for the activities of the priest who is a professional, there need be no dilemma.[15] The fact is, however, that a conflict of roles often exists, and contrasting obligations have led some to abandon their religious commitment.

Sometimes there is a conflict because the professional expertise of the individual is disdained by colleagues or superiors. The highly trained professional is not appreciated by the bishop or the superior who makes the appointments of subordinates. The sister who did brilliant graduate work and earned a doctorate in philosophy is sent to teach children in an elementary school. This kind of experience is said to develop the virtue of humility. It is indeed a test of obedience and an antidote to pride to be asked to set aside one's hard-earned professional qualifications.

Bishops and other religious superiors who underwrite the professional training and education of their subordinates may not always be aware that they are opening the way to alternative careers. Motivation is complex and multiple, and it should not be assumed that anyone deliberately takes advantage of professional education in order to prepare for an economically viable exodus from a church occupation. Nevertheless, one study has shown that, among women religious, the orders with

107

the higher educational levels among their members had the higher rates of leaving.[16]

Credibility of the Church

Most of the people who resign their church vocation remain members of the Catholic Church. Among the resignees responding to the bishops' survey more than half (fifty-six percent) still consider themselves to be priests, and almost eight out of ten (seventy-eight percent) acknowledge their membership in the Catholic Church. James Kavanaugh on occasion viciously attacked the Church, and once wrote: "No longer will I accept in silence the travesties that a dishonest theology has imposed on simple and unsuspecting men. Nor will I leave the Church, even if they demand it of me, for it is my Church."[17]

When we hear that lay people "lose the faith," we usually understand that they no longer attend mass; they are said to be fallen away from the Church and the sacraments. But only a small proportion (twelve percent) of resigned priests say that one of their reasons for leaving the priesthood was a serious doubt about faith. It is necessary to distinguish faith in God from acceptance of the theological and moral teachings of the Church. Thirty-five percent of the resigned priests said that a "very important" reason for their leaving the ministry was disagreement with some ethical or moral teaching of the church. In most instances, this moral teaching was the 1968 encyclical, *Humanae Vitae*. This was the obstacle that Bishop James Shannon could not surmount; he could not, he said, keep two sets of books, "privately believing one thing but having to teach another. I cannot in conscience give internal assent, much less external assent, to the papal teaching in question."

While James Shannon continues his adherence to the

church as a supportive lay parishioner, Charles Davis, the British theologian, does not (although he remains a Christian with no denominational affiliation). Davis said that "for me, Christian commitment is inseparable from concern for truth and concern for people. I do not find either of these represented by the official church. There is a concern for authority at the expense of truth, and I am constantly saddened by instances of the damage done to persons by workings of an impersonal and unfree system."[18]

Studies do show that terminators among the clergy are oriented to change, and are much more likely to question the credibility of the institutional church than most other people. Resigned priests are three times as likely to want a restructuring of church government as they are to want a chance for optional celibacy.[19]

Love and Loneliness

Mutual concern and familial relationships are said to be characteristic of the Catholic priesthood, and especially of clergy and brothers and sisters belonging to religious communities. Yet a priest who resigned from one religious congregation wrote that "the old saying about being lonely in a crowd is really true, and it can be just as true for a priest in a religious order as for anyone else. It was certainly so in my case, and I do not hesitate to name loneliness as the prime reason for my leaving the religious life."[20]

Misuse of authority is a greater concern; when priests in the active ministry were asked about the problems facing them and their fellow priests they were twice as likely to mention authority as to mention loneliness. "But it is loneliness that predicts more strongly the propensity to leave the priesthood."[21] John Haag found in his in-depth interviews with members of *Corpus* that the problems of authority and celibacy, encountered after ordination, may have their source in the failure of the individual in the seminary to develop maturity. Haag's interviews tend to reflect the psychological interpretations of priestly immaturity discussed by Kennedy and Heckler in their 1972 study, *The Catholic Priest in the United States: Psychological Investigations.*[22]

When administrators of one hundred and seventy-four religious communities of men were asked why members left, the question of loneliness was not even raised. Seven out of ten, however, listed preference for marriage, and problems with celibacy, as the most frequent reasons members left the order.[23] A study of women religious who had taken final vows before leaving found a lower proportion (fifty-two percent) who had a preference for marriage.[24] And the data on the number who actually marry after leaving the convent support the thesis that marriage is not a major factor in why women leave the religious life.[25]

Some of the former priests are quite forthright in expressing the linkage of loneliness, love and marriage. One diocesan priest recounts that "I wanted the archbishop to know that I was offering him my resignation for one reason only: I wanted to marry." He said that he was reluctant to resign, and he "was not resigning because of the priesthood, but because of celibacy." In gradute studies at Catholic University he had received a "re-education" in the new theology. As a result, "I became aware that I was far more isolated in the world than I ought to be, or would like to be. When I finally realized how alone I was . . . I realized that I was teaching and preaching one thing and living another."[26] Pope Paul VI showed a certain sympathy for the isolation of the priest in his encyclical on *Sacerdotal Celibacy*, when he talked about "the human loneliness of the priest, which is so often the cause of his discouragement and temptation."

The Counter-Culture

The massive exodus of church personnel cannot adequately be explained if it is seen simply as a behavior problem brought on by individual decisions. The late 1960s was the time of student dissatisfaction and campus upheaval, of women's liberation and the National Organization for Women, of the civil rights movement and the fight for racial justice. Picket lines and peace marches attracted the support of religious sisters. "Feminist thought took root in American religious communities during the period of renewal," notes one commentator,[27] "and it was impossible not to see how the feminist critique applied to church institutions."

Lucinda SanGiovanni, in her in-depth study of former sisters, found both an *ideological* "push" out of the convent, as a consequence of the enormous changes taking place in religious life, and a *personal* "pull" toward the options they now had as women—options that were unavailable to them as long as they remained nuns.[28]

Nevertheless, people do react differently to changes in the social structure, and do not mechanically and uniformly respond to the "push or pull" sequence. Sister Marie Augusta Neal, whose data on sisters' resignations come from administrators who have personal knowledge of the leavers, is of the opinion that "in all probability, the overall trends in numbers leaving are more social than psychic." They are caused, she says, "by concomitant trends in the conditions of society and the church's response to them, the changing apostolic needs in relation to population shifts, and new calls for prophetic and institutional service."[29] The psychic attraction to the orderly routine of prayer and contemplation was often out of harmony with the demands of social ministry among the poor and underprivileged. The church itself was responding to the "signs of the times," and neither the church nor the convent would ever be the same again.

A significant after-effect of these cultural changes was that the departure from the priesthood, and especially from the convent, was no longer deemed an act of immorality. The church vocation has not completely lost its sacred aura, but the decision to seek exclaustration has become almost commonplace. There appears to be a kind of psychological momentum in the sheer numbers who have elected to go secular. The choice of an alternative vocation and lifestyle which had been "unthinkable" previously now becomes thinkable when so many have made the choice.

While friends and relatives may be saddened by one's decision to leave, there is no longer a general condemnation of the resignee as a derelict, a deserter, a deviant. Hernan Vera[30] found that practicing priests tend to give positive ratings to resigned priests. For the most part the stigma of defection has been removed from both ex-priests and ex-nuns, who mingle today almost unnoticed in the Catholic population. They are often employed in diocesan offices, parishes, schools, and hospitals under the auspices of the church—a type of employment that would have been unthinkable a generation ago.

Postscript: "The day I signed my indult of secularization I had been a professed nun for thirty-one years. Why do nuns leave? Why, in the end, did I leave religious life? Mainly because I had come to realize that I had grown into quite another person from the twenty-two-year-old girl who once felt compelled to follow a vocation and dedicate myself to Catholic education. Today I am convinced that God has really no plan for me other than the one I evolve for myself. Since I feel able to grow more fully as a person outside the structure of religious life, then that is His will for me."[31]

1. Jackson Carroll and Robert Wilson, *Too Many Pastors? The Clergy Job Market.* New York: Pilgrim Press, 1980.

2. Robert Merton, "Insiders and Outsiders," *American Journal of Sociology*, July, 1972, 78, pp. 9–47.

3. Everett Hughes, *Men and Their Work.* Glencoe: Free Press, 1958, pp. 158–159.

4. Joseph H. Fichter, *Religion as an Occupation.* University of Notre Dame Press, 1961, p. 205. One resignee admitted he was at fault. "Since we are taught in theology that sufficient grace, or help from God, is given to each priest to enable him to carry out his commitment, obviously I had failed to cooperate with His grace." George L. Weber, "I Heard A Voice," p. 157, in John A. O'Brien, *Why Priests Leave.* New York: Hawthorn, 1969.

5. "An Enquiry About Vocations," pp. 75–76.

6. Marie Augusta Neal, *Catholic Sisters in Transition.* Wilmington: Glazier, 1984, p. 22.

7. Helen Rose Ebaugh, *Out of the Cloister.* Austin: University of Texas Press, 1977, p. 109.

8. Monica Baldwin, *I Leap Over the Wall.* New York: Rinehart, 1950, pp. vi, 301. She suggested an alternative title, "Impressions of a Square Peg in a Round Hole."

9. Joseph H. Fichter, *America's Forgotten Priests.* New York: Harper & Row, 1968, p. 231.

10. Robert M. Duggan, "Not Really Leaving," pp. 47–57, in John A. O'Brien, *Why Priests Leave.* New York: Hawthorn, 1969.

11. This is a liberal ecclesial interpretation of Douglas Hall and Benjamin Schneider, *Organizational Climates and Careers: The Work Lives of Priests.* New York: Seminar Press, 1983, p. 162.

12. Jeannine Grammick, "From Good Sisters to Pro-

JOSEPH H. FICHTER, S.J.

phetic Women," pp. 226–237, in Ann Patrick Ware, ed., *Midwives of the Future*. Kansas City: Leaven Press, 1985.

13. See Arthur F. LeBlanc, "I'm Not Lonely Now," pp. 35–46, in John A. O'Brien, op. cit.

14. The first and most thorough survey answered by resigned clergy themselves is reported in chapter 15, "A Look at the Resignees," pp. 275–309, *The Catholic Priest in the United States: Sociological Investigations*. Washington: United States Catholic Conference, 1972.

15. See "The Myth of the Hyphenated Clergy," pp. 15–32, in William H. Cleary, ed., *Hyphenated Clergy*. Washington: Corpus Books, 1969.

16. Ebaugh, op. cit., p. 91. Resigned priests, especially those in religious orders, are much more likely to have earned post-graduate academic degrees. *Sociological Investigations*, op. cit., p. 42.

17. James Kavanaugh, *A Modern Priest Looks at His Out-Dated Church*. New York: Trident Press, 1967, p. 179.

18. Charles Davis, *A Question of Conscience*. New York: Harper & Row, 1967, p. 7.

19. *Sociological Investigations*, op. cit, p. 301.

20. Le Blanc, op. cit., p. 36.

21. *Sociological Investigations*, op. cit., pp. 206–214.

22. John E. Haag, *A Study of the Seminary and Priesthood Experience of Thirteen Resigned Roman Catholic Priests*. Doctoral Paper, Pittsburgh Theological Seminary, 1984. See also Eugene Kennedy and Victor Heckler, *The Catholic Priest in the United States: Psychological Investigations*. Washington: USCC, 1972.

23. Joseph Shields and Mary Verdieck, *Religious Life in the United States*. Washington: CARA, 1985, p. 13.

24. Marie Augusta Neal, op. cit., p. 22. In the judgment of administrators, the preference for marriage jumped from twenty percent in 1966 to fifty-two percent in 1982.

114

25. Ebaugh, op. cit., p. 111.

26. George Frein, "For the Love of Jeanne," pp. 85–98, in O'Brien, op. cit.

27. Kaye Ashe, "Looking Back, Looking Ahead," pp. 218–225, in Ann Ware, op. cit.

28. Lucinda SanGiovanni, *Ex-Nuns: A Study of Emergent Role Passage*. Norwood: Ablex, 1968, Chapter 3, "Making the Decision To Leave."

29. Marie Augusta Neal, op. cit., p. 23.

30. Hernan Vera, *The Professionalization and Professionalism of Catholic Priests*. Gainesville: University Presses of Florida, 1982, p. 84.

31. Mary Griffin, *The Courage To Choose*. Boston: Little, Brown, 1975, p. 200.

Adult Commitment at Century's End: Some Technological Influences

John M. Staudenmaier, S.J.

Jesus said: "In the evening you say, 'It will be fine; there is a red sky,' and in the morning, 'Stormy weather today; the sky is red and overcast.' You know how to read the face of the sky, but you cannot read the signs of the times" (Mt 16:2).

In this essay I try to read three signs of our times. First, in the twentieth century a set of complex technologies—the telephone, radio-television, automobiles, nuclear weapons, computers and so forth—have come to structure the nation's life and to influence our personal, communal, and civic lives. Second, this same set of technologies has recently begun to show signs of a crisis in America's technological style. Third, we see a striking change in the way Americans experience adult commitment, a change reflected in the accelerated divorce rate and in the dramatic decline of entrants to religious life over the past twenty years. Unlikely as it may seem at first glance, all three signs of the times are related.

A Changing Culture

To begin we might keep some interesting patterns in mind.[1] In 1910 America's divorce rate stood at 8.8% of marriages attempted. The seventy year climb to today's 50% rate

116

does not describe a consistent curve over the time. Marriage failures actually declined during the depression (from 17.3 to 16.5%) but in the tumult of World War II's ending they leaped to 30%, a then all-time high. After settling back into the mid twenty percent range, divorces gradually climbed back to 32.7% in 1970 and then soared to an astonishing 50.3% in 1976, a neighborhood it has occupied ever since.

Recent divorce figures parallel a similar trend in religious vocations. Studies by Neal and Shields-Verdieck indicate that entrants to religious life have declined by approximately 75% over the past two decades.[2]

These patterns reveal a culture that is deeply, and recently, troubled about commitments that are both communal and enduring. Declining numbers are worrisome. Besides forcing major changes in ministerial style, they tempt us to doubt that vowed religious life remains viable. More significantly, however, American troubles with commitment tell us something important about the women and men who risk religious life today and about United States culture generally.

It could be argued that these trends reflect nothing more serious than a significant shift in the way Americans understand and live their commitments, and that demographic changes—in particular increased life span—and social changes—in particular geographical mobility, greater affluence, and a dramatically broadened array of career options for men and women at every age—have led more and more Americans to opt for a series of temporary commitments, any one of which is subject to critique and replacement. It would be foolhardy to discount such interpretations and indeed such is not my intent. On the other hand, I do not find it complete as an explanation. Taken alone, the rationality implied by this interpretation misses several key dimensions of the commitment phenomenon as we find it today.

JOHN M. STAUDENMAIER, S.J.

A Crisis of Personal Values and Emotions

Men and women rarely, if ever, experience divorce or departure from religious life as a primarily rational act. Such choices declare bankruptcy on one of the most significant decisions of adult life. They often evoke deeply felt grief, fear, anger, or guilt. Even more telling, in my experience, young adults often experience strong anxiety when facing a binding commitment, temporary or permanent. Something more goes on here than a calculated, rational response to changing societal conditions. In what follows, I will suggest that these troubles with communal commitment are one symptom of a society in crisis. Every stable culture provides, among other things, a coherent world view which renders adult commitment believable. We Americans may well live in one of those times when our society faces the challenge of renegotiating its cultural world view, of finding our way to a new consensus about adulthood, both its opportunities and its responsibilities.[3]

Such a major cultural shift cannot be explained by any single cause. Thus, if we were to flatten the divorce curve over the century we could argue persuasively that American troubles with the marriage commitment reflect the growing influence of therapeutic and self-centered individualism and a correlative decline in our capacity to base our lives on shared consensus about the common good.[4] On the other hand, we might explain the first surge in the divorce rate as a result of forces set in motion by World War II and the second surge, after 1965, in terms of a host of factors (the flower children, the Vietnam War, Watergate, etc.) which have eroded American trust in established institutions generally. Neal, and Shields-Verdieck, and other studies in this volume explain declining religious vocations in terms of Vatican II and related changes in religious congregations and the church. All these interpretations have considerable merit. In this essay,

118

however, I will explore a less frequently considered dimension of our cultural context. I will argue here that we can deepen our understanding of American culture and our current commitment troubles by paying attention to our technological style, asking as we do so how the values embedded in that style influence our experience of commitment.

Our technological style flourished through much of this century until, due partly to the powerful catalytic influence of World War II, it entered a period of crisis somewhere in the 1960s. The limitations of our technological style suggest some of the causes of its own crisis even as they provide a partial explanation of how commitment has become problematic in the recent past. Finally, both the limitations and the strengths of our twentieth century technological style provide us with some clues that can assist our efforts to help young people who are called to join us and to help one another live our own commitments.

Technological Style and Adult Commitment

No successful technology—not the moving assembly line, not nuclear power plants, not television, not even a new cosmetic—ever came into being as a result of "inevitable progress." Human beings with their tangled motives decide which designs are attended to and which ignored. Real people decide why the technologies found worthy of inventive attention take the final shape they do. This maxim, the central tenet of contextual history of technology, provides a basis for understanding "technological style."[5] Because a technical design reflects the motives of its design constituency, historians of technology look to the values, biases, motives and world view of the designers when asked why a given technology turned out as it did. Every technology, then, embodies some distinct set of values. To the extent that a technology becomes successful within its society, its inherent values will be reinforced. In this sense, every technology carries its own "style," fostering some values while inhibiting others. In the technological view of history, tradeoffs abound. There is no technological free lunch.[6]

Technological style causes as well as reflects values. Just as America adapted to the automobile in a host of ways from new highway funding legislation to shopping malls, so every society adapts to the designs of its successful technologies. In the process, the values that fit the technologies achieve societal momentum while values that do not fit diminish in importance.

So important are successful technologies in shaping societal structures and fostering cultural values, that when a once successful technological style becomes obsolescent, its host society faces a major crisis. Such, I believe, is our situation in America today.[7] If I am right, it should not surprise us to see signs of crisis in all aspects of American culture including the capacity for enduring, communal commitment.

Memberships Chosen and Unchosen

Before turning to the sketch of America's twentieth century technological style let us consider two personal traits— durable personal identity and the capacity for communal life— that are central to commitment. Whether I like it or not, my life is structured by the groups into which I am born— familial, local, ethnic, religious, or national. Membership is not optional; they are part of the givens of birth. When I make an *adult* commitment, however, I enter a community that, from my point of view at least, need never have existed. This freely chosen involvement, so unlike the inevitable bonds of infancy, requires a capacity for communal living and confidence in my personal identity.

I do not engage in a life-shaping commitment on the spur

of the moment. Some series of events leads me to believe that this person or this congregation is "for me." To move from uncommitted outsider to committed member I must come to see that series of events as blessed, the beginnings of a communal life story wherein my individualistic "I" gradually becomes part of a "we." As long as the events remain disconnected episodes I remain a lone wanderer. Only as I recognize the pattern that they form can I imagine that these events and the person or community central to them might become key elements of my adult identity. Permanent commitment, then, is less a prediction of my future than an act of belief in my history. I believe that the fabric woven of these blessed events will hold through the uncertainties that will surely come as I and those to whom I commit myself live communal life.

For the choice to be rooted in Christian faith I must come to see the blessed events not only as uniting me with some person or community, but also as the fabric of a vocation. For a Christian, God is the one who leads on the journey of faith. The community of the church grows out of faith in the Lord Jesus and expresses itself in our adult commitments to one another.[8] I am less concerned here, however, with our belief that Christian commitments are rooted in God's call than with a prior question, our inner capacity for binding adult commitment of any sort.

One major change in recent American culture seems to be the replacement of stable expectations for the future by a radical uncertainty about the changes that will come. Young people today seem acutely aware of the storms Jesus took to be inevitable in his parable of the house built on sand or rock (Mt 7:24). They show less confidence in their ability to find the rock on which to build. "What do I need," they seem to ask, "if I am even to imagine myself engaging in an enduring and communal faith commitment?" Counseling young adults has suggested two key characteristics. First, I must trust my identity, believing that my inner life can be the source of a life story that will endure, that my life-events and my choices are not disconnected episodes, shifting like the sands on which Jesus' ill-fated house was built. Second, I must have the capacity to grow from the individualism of the outsider into the bonds of community, at once so liberating and so constraining.

Keeping these two characteristics in mind, let us turn to a sketch of America's technological style, asking first, "How do the values of that style affect my sense of personal identity?" and second, "How does that style affect my capacity for communal life?"

Personal and Communal Identity: Some American Tensions

For historians causal explanation resembles the wire strands of a cable more than the links of a chain. In a chain-link argument every event must "prove" the next; the whole weight of the argument rests on each segment. Because of the complexity of their subject matter, historians look for trends, for events which, like the strands in a cable, reinforce one another.[9] Rarely does a historian argue that "this and only this caused that." While I will note some positive American technological values that foster commitment, I will stress the negative. This reflects the primary purpose of this essay: to consider a few strands in the cable of factors that make adult commitment so difficult today.

Systemic Standardization Replaces Negotiation

Until 1870 or so the challenge of conquering the wilderness shaped the dominant technological style in the United States. As generations of men and women from Europe or the more settled eastern United States headed west, their longing for a "middle landscape," a livable place carved out of the wild, grew into a central element of the American character.

Building a human place, clearing fields and rivers, constructing homes, roads, canals, bridges, tunnels, and cities preoccupied the technological imagination. Americans honored technical expertise as "knowhow," a blend of often crude rules of thumb, occasional engineering elegance, courage, and an intimate knowledge of local terrain, as the context whose constraints defined the limits of every project. Technological style, then, demanded a continual negotiation between the skills, tools, and plans of white Americans and the godlike wilderness they sought to conquer.[10] Despite their passion for freedom and individualism, Americans found negotiation a basic necessity in human interaction as well. People needed one another in an empty land.

Long before this technological style fell from preeminence a successor began to exert its influence. Beginning in 1815 with the U.S. Ordnance Department's commitment to standardized uniformity in weapons production, a new technical ideal was gathering momentum in the land.[11] The new ideal embodied a radical shift in values. The older style's negotiation with nature and with co-workers shifted toward standardization's precision design and centralized authority. The new American factory system turned out a host of new products, and in the process transformed the relationship between manager and worker from the sometimes respectful and sometimes tumultuous interaction of the early American small shop to heavy-handed enforcement of work rules coupled with the de-skilling of workers through increasingly automated machines.[12] The transformation was hardly limited to the factory. Little by little, a broad range of technological endeavors began to adopt the standardization ideal. Consider, for example, the railroads.

The geographical range and managerial complexity of the railroads fostered standardization in many ways. The railroads' need for precise timetables transformed a land of multi-

123

ple, local times into 1885's single system of standard time divided into our now familiar four time zones. The depot, that little building where town and rail line met, gradually evolved toward a standardized architecture, thus reflecting the triumph of railroad system over local style. The telegraph, essential as an information component for the rail lines, soon became the vehicle for nationwide, standardized news with the development of the wire services.[13]

We see the same trend in the changing character of electrical systems. Our dependence on electicity, together with the complex requirements of generation and transmission systems, has changed the earlier negotiated relationship to one of conformity.[14]

A major redefinition of advertising, just after World War I, extends the pattern. The new style tried to program consumer emotions, creating a sense of personal inadequacy and discontent as the basis of impulse buying. In a way, consumerist advertising is the epitome of standardization's triumph over negotiation. The new form of marketing tried to extend standardized conformity into human motivation itself.[15]

These three examples indicate a radical shift of the values embedded in our normal technologies. The word "technology" once meant "the tools and techniques that humans make and use for their purposes." Our twentieth century style reflects a new definition of our most complex technologies: "elegantly designed systems on which we depend for our survival." Twentieth century systems tend to resolve the old problem of peers negotiating with one another by bringing once independent negotiators inside the system as functional components.

Standardization yields substantial benefits. Standardized mass production permits a much larger segment of the population to own relatively high quality manufactured goods improving the standard of living for poor as well as rich. Even more important, standardization fosters and rewards the virtue of precision. Living as we do in an age where elegant systems such as telephone networks, electric utilities, medical technologies, and computers are commonplace, we find it hard to imagine a world where the art of making steel seemed almost magical. Precision design has joined the family of the elegant arts even as it makes possible the systems on which our communication, our health, and our productivity depend.

With its many virtues, however, standardization carries significant liabilities; most important for us is the atrophy of negotiation. Negotiation is a messy business. When mutually independent peers must find a common way of proceeding, their different world views, vested interests, and styles make the outcome unpredictable whether the people in question are skilled workers and managers, shoppers and sellers, or independent nations. In the quest for a common good no one participant's version of the best solution will be adopted. Despite its inefficiencies, the interdependence inherent in negotiation requires and therefore fosters a capacity for intimacy with others not like myself and an abiding sense of the value of agenda other than my own.[16]

Two Questions

(1) What are the challenges for adult commitment in a standardized culture? Presently we are tempted to take precision elegance for granted. We tend to forget that complex systems are human achievements, that the labor of human beings, trained in a tradition of excellence, maintain them as they work their wonders.

Such amnesia has serious consequences even in the realm of adult commitment. When we forget that our systems are the work of human beings, they seem to acquire a godlike inevitability and we begin to feel like dwarfs in their presence. "What difference do I make in a world dominated by these massive technologies?" Even the technically competent among us can suffer from these feelings of inadequacy. Outside our areas of expertise all of us depend on technologies beyond our comprehension. But adult commitments require a deep confidence in our creative power. To make a binding life commitment we must believe that we can create a life story whose meaning makes life's struggle worthwhile.

(2) We can turn the standardization-negotiation relationship around and ask a second question. Are we Americans, schooled in a whole host of conforming patterns and unschooled in the difficult process of negotiation, tempted to relate to one another and to God in the same fashion? Insofar as commitment to a religious community is an adult act and not just a search for security, a religious embraces lifelong negotiation with the rest of the community. We enter in the hope that we have identities so vital that each of us makes a difference to the rest.

The American tendency to replace negotiation with standardized conformity creates a serious imbalance in our society. It challenges us to find ways to recover our ability to embrace the unpredictability of negotiation. Standardization's precision and negotiation's uncertainties seem to work best in creative tension, each with the other.

Absolutized Light and the "Holy Dark"

Before the electric light, people lived a diurnal rhythm alternating between light and dark. Night was a culturally experienced reality, a time of sleep, intimacy, and storytelling, but not, one prayed, a time of crisis when poor artificial light left people nearly helpless. Electric lights have soothed our ancient night fears but they have also realized the dream of the eighteenth century divines and that turns out to be a mixed blessing. With high quality light we can now do almost anything—from grading papers to repairing freeways—in any of the twenty-four hours of the day. Lacking a common "night" to stop us all at the same time, we tend to squeeze more and more into our days.

What happens to a culture that loses the night? Imagine for a moment that we were to "fast" from electricity— telephone, radio, television, stereo, computer, and electric lights—one night a week. How would it influence us once we had gotten over its novelty and settled into a weekly rhythm? The absence of electricity's networks would foster leisure for many forms of intimacy. We might tell stories by candlelight, sharing the events of the week with their passion and ordinariness. We could have a party, but human beings would provide the sounds of merriment. We might sit still in contemplation. Or we could retire early and enter the mystery of sleep gently. Unlike our ancestors we would celebrate these virtues of the holy dark with little fear that crisis might shatter our tranquility. If needed, the electric lights are at hand. Would such a rhythm, a real "night" one night a week, be imaginable? Would a good American want to drop out of the fast pace of life in this fashion? Not readily, I suspect.

Avoidance of the night symbolizes but hardly exhausts every aspect of our fear of the dark.

Darkness, Light and Commitment

How does fear of the dark influence commitment? It does so by driving people toward light—in this case, the light of scrutiny. Contemporary society honors scrutiny of existing relationships, and, more than most cultures, acknowledges the value of changing what needs to be changed. Effort aimed at such improvements nuances the original commitment— hopefully for the better. But the very effort has its risks, its ambiguities. When does God call us to endure the burdens and self-sacrifice of a present commitment, when to abandon it as unsalvageable? We cannot avoid the question.

We may be helped to discern our commitments by learning to think of light and dark as a creative tension. The life stories we craft with our adult commitments demand an alternation of journeys in the light and journeys in the dark.

Relentless clarity kills adult commitment. We cannot avoid the uncertainty inherent in negotiating our changing relationships. Close friendships in religious life call for the same reverence with dark times that marriage does. A commitment to learning involves long periods of confusion before we achieve genuine understanding. For religious, as for everyone else, these dark journeys are an essential dimension of the human rhythm of life. A culture dishonors them to its peril.

Electronic Interaction Replaces Sensual Interaction

The old style of living in our neighborhoods, of homes with spacious front porches, has been replaced, by and large, by a less physical mode of interaction. The telephone alone, of course, is not responsible for the trend. Automobiles have tended to replace mass transit and, while both have their unpleasant aspects during rush hour, the automobile insulates us from the bodies of our fellow travelers. On the other hand, radio and television have created a style of human discourse—pre-packaged, highly crafted, passively received, and electronically disseminated—which competes with spontaneous human interaction. The child for whom television is a baby sitter learns to doubt whether he or she can be the source of talk that matters.

I wonder whether our culture's stress on genital sexuality is not, in part at least, a reflection of our sensual deprivation. For a people who are starving for touch on so many ordinary levels of interaction, genital sexuality has come to be one of our few remaining ways to live up to Ma Bell's ironic invitation to "reach out and touch someone."

Much more could be said about electronic technologies and permanent commitment. We have just scratched the surface of this kind of technological contemplation. But in this short essay we must consider one final piece of the technology-commitment puzzle. America's technological style, with all its strengths and weaknesses, appears to have entered a stage of crisis in the recent past.

Since World War II: Commitment and Hope

World War II seems to signal the beginning of several powerful social transformations that would lead not only to America's technological crisis, but also to the global-personal character of hope and despair experienced by young adults today.

The war set in motion a series of events—technological, economic, political, and symbolic—that created a global consciousness that is new for Americans and, indeed, for the human race. At the same time, the war served as a catalyst, bringing together the various strands of America's technological ideal of standardization and precision, amplifying their force in such a way that their tendency to erode our capacity for adult commitment reached crisis proportions.

Six Phenomena

Let us consider six events: (1) World War II itself, (2) the constantly expanding array of nuclear weapons, (3) the exploration of space, (4) the worldwide communications network, (5) recent evidence that our technical systems begin to put pressure on global ecological resources, and (6) unmistakable signs that America is no longer "number one" militarily or economically.

World War II was fought in every major area of the world

except, perhaps, Latin America. Most Americans knew friends or kin who risked their lives in exotic places like Burma, Guadalcanal, North Africa and Europe. Concern for them forced our national attention past continental boundaries.

The atomic bomb may be our most powerful post-war symbol. This new weapon can destroy the planet and not just one city; it forces us to imagine our whole frame of reference exploding.[17]

Space travel reinforces the shift from local to global consciousness. Exquisite photos called attention, as nothing previous could, to the beauty of the earth as a single planet—and a small one at that.

Since the war, world communications networks (air travel, telephone, radio-television-satellite, and computer) have created an economic and political world order woven together in a web of mutual causalities. The radio-television network forces us to pay attention.

Increasing international awareness of natural resource limits, such as water shortages, deforestation, and toxic pollution, begins to make us see systemic technological expansion as an ecological problem of planetary rather than local or even national dimensions.

Finally, Americans have recently begun to realize that we may no longer be "number one" militarily or economically, and we find this unsettling. We saw ourselves after World War II as the planet's benefactors. At great national sacrifice, we had defeated two enemies whom we saw to be demonic and, in the process, saved the world for democracy. A return to domestic abundance enhanced the heady excitement of war's end.

Gradually, however, our circumstances have changed. Russia, motivated in part by its traditional paranoia, has achieved rough military parity. New industrial centers, Japan being the most noteworthy, have rebuilt from the war's ruins to challenge our technological supremacy in area after area.

We are shocked to learn that American "know-how" no longer leads the world.

Small, Troubled World

Throughout our history and almost without our noticing it, America's technological success depended on the nation's splendid isolation. Our technological style emerged in a massive land so extraordinarily endowed with natural resources and so empty of any history deemed worthy of notice that we assumed unlimited expansion as a national birthright. But the very expansion of those systems that now unite the planet, and our technological style's erosion of the will to negotiate, have finally caught up with us. Americans must learn to negotiate with one another, with the natural environment, and with our planetary neighbors. We cannot foresee the outcome and that frightens us.

Despair, Hope and Adult Commitment

How might we interpret these signs of the times? Taken together, it seems to me, they invite us to live in hope just as much as they tempt us to despair. Because our world has grown so much closer together we are called to a hope, at once personal and global in its scope. For us members of the church, the signs of our times reveal, as in no previous era of history, the extraordinary daring of Jesus' invitation to "go out into the whole world and bring the good news to all creation."[18]

Many young people who seek religious life today come because they have been inspired by the nobility of Jesus' call to work for the healing of the whole world. But they do not come unmarked by the struggle with despair. Despair tempts us all in the form of a numb passivity that inclines us to withdraw from effective commitment to the larger challenges of our society and our world. Despair, too, helps explain the anxiety which these young people feel when they face adult commitment. A generation ago it may have been possible to enter the religious life because a ghetto Catholic culture rewarded the move with high social status. Such a religious could grow into the vision of Jesus as the years passed. Today, however, when religious life has lost much of its social status luster, many who consider a vocation face the stark challenges of the vowed life at the outset. "Can I make a commitment that lasts? Can I engage in the lifelong intimacy of prayer and community? Can I respond to Jesus' love for the whole world in a way that makes a difference to that world?" The questions run deep indeed. There is no simple recipe for encouraging commitment but I would like to make three suggestions, drawn from the analysis just completed:

1. *Pay attention to the force of technologically-based imbalances.*

Whether I face my responsibility as a citizen of a society in crisis or the more personal call to enter adult community, it helps me to expect that the value imbalances of my culture will challenge the hope on which these commitments depend. The more I am aware of my own temptations as one who embodies the values of his culture, the more I can support and encourage others who desire and nevertheless fear adult commitment.

2. *Respect the struggle with hope and despair.*

I read somewhere that St. Ignatius, the founder of my own order, preferred candidates who need a bridle to those who need spurs. He would not, I suspect, see a young adult deeply moved by hope and tempted to despair as unsuitable for the society. If we avoid the vulnerability and confusion of the inner journey we run the risk of driving vital and gifted young adults from our midst or of encouraging premature conformity. Such a short-cut can lead to a life of sterile rigidity or postpone the encounter with hope and despair until it erupts in later life. Neither outcome represents the charism of the vowed life.

3. *Honor storytelling and make time for it.*

Storytelling is not a form of entertainment that radio and television have rendered obsolete. When we set aside time to tell each other the details of our life, our good and bad news, we embody the profound and simple hope that intimacy stands at the heart of life and commitment. To recover the art of storytelling we will have to risk being countercultural. The suggestion of fasting from electricity may be more than a heuristic device aimed at revealing our addiction to that technology. One night a week dedicated to staying home and telling one another our stories—a practice that many religious have begun through the structure of small support groups—might transform our communal lives. It would help heal the temptation to show only our strengths while hiding the ambiguous and vulnerable core of our humanity.

Could it be, then, that the complex relationship between America's technological style and the crisis of commitment comes down to the challenge of intimacy? I think so. As mature adults, we will embrace our commitments if we are willing to balance conformity with negotiation and the clarity of light with the mystery of the dark. Finally, as followers of Jesus, we will respond to his commitment to the world's healing if we risk intimacy with our world, our sisters and brothers, and our inner journey of faith. In the process we have good reason to hope that others will continue to be called to join us and that we will have the inner resources to welcome them.

Notes

1. For data cited in this paragraph see *Historical Statistics of the U.S.*

2. Marie Augusta Neal, SND de Namur, *Catholic Sisters in Transition: From the 1960's to the 1980's* (Wilmington, Delaware: Michael Glazier, Inc. 1984) and Joseph J. Shields and Mary Jeanne Verdieck, *Religious Life in the United States: The Experience of Men's Communities* (Washington, D.C.: Center for Applied Research in the Apostolate, 1985).

3. The success of the Jesuit Volunteer Corps and similar groups at Maryknoll and elsewhere suggests that commitment troubles do not spring from a decline in generous desires to say "yes" to God's redeeming love for the world. The volunteer structure works precisely because it permits young adults to exercise their generous desires in a non-permanent way. The year-long experience helps volunteers grow in the belief that a life shaped by permanent commitments to faith and justice is possible. Still the JVC knows that it flies in the face of the culture just as novice directors know the society does. The JVC's playful-serious motto is "ruined for life." For these men and women, as for Jesuit novices, the question of commitment is as frightening as it is central.

4. See also *Habits of the Heart* (Berkeley: Univ. of California Press, 1985) where Robert Bellah, Richard Madsen, William Sullivan, Ann Swidler, and Steven Tipton present persuasive evidence of America's need to renegotiate a vision of the common good.

5. The argument is complex. For a full elaboration see my *Technology's Storytellers: Reweaving the Human Fabric.* Cambridge, MA: The MIT Press, 1985, especially Chapter 1.

6. On the tradeoffs inherent in technological style, see Thomas P. Hughes, "We Get the Technology We Deserve," *American Heritage,* October–November 1985, pp. 65–79.

7. For a vivid portrayal of America's technological crisis, see Francis Ford Coppola's *Koyaanisqatsi.* The film title is a Hopi noun meaning "a situation out of control that requires change."

8. Christian commitment as vocation, so pervasive in both the Old and New Testament stories of respond to God's call, is elegantly articulated by John Dunne. "God is not 'how things stand.' 'How things stand' is not God. God is not domesticated by 'how things stand.' God leads on an adventure. God is wild." *The Reasons of the Heart: A Journey into Solitude and Back Again into the Human Circle* (New York: Macmillan Publishing Co., 1978), p. 21.

9. I am indebted to the late Dr. James Collins who, long ago in a philosophy class at St. Louis University, introduced me to this distinction.

10. Carolyn Merchant's *The Death of Nature: Women, Ecology, and the Scientific Revolution* (New York: Harper & Row, 1980) traces the gradual shift, in Western Europe, from nature defined as the goddess who sets the rules and boundaries for human enterprise to a still feminine but newly passive reality destined for exploitation and conquest. As early Americans encountered the virgin wilderness they found their heritage of conquest tempered as much by nature's raw beauty and power as by the crudity of their tools.

For other discussions of the middle landscape see Leo Marx, *The Machine in the Garden: Technology and the Pastoral Idea in America* (New York: Oxford, 1964), John F. Kasson, *Civilizing the Machine: Technology and Republican Values in America, 1776–1900* (New York: Penguin Books, 1976), and Thomas Merton *Conjectures of a Guilty Bystander* (New York: Doubleday, 1968), pp. 33–39.

11. For a careful study of the drive toward standardization in the Ordnance Department see Merritt Roe Smith, "Military Enterprise and Innovative Process," in M. R. Smith, ed., *Military Enterprise and Technological Change: Perspectives on the American Experience* (Cambridge, MA: The MIT Press, 1985).

12. The most helpful single source on changing labor-management relations in America is Herbert Gutman's *Work,*

Culture and Society in Industrializing America (New York: Vintage, 1966).

13. Carlene Stephens, *Inventing Standard Time*, Washington, DC: The Smithsonian Institution, 1983. On the telegraph wire services, see Daniel J. Czitrom, *Media and the American Mind: From Morse to McLuhan* (Chapel Hill: University of North Carolina Press, 1982), Ch. 1. Mark Duluk, "The American Railroad Depot as Technological Vernacular Architecture," in *Dichotomy*, Vol. 5, No. 1 (Spring 1982), pp. 10–15.

14. For a definitive study of electrification in the United States, Germany and Great Britain see Thomas Parke Hughes, *Networks of Power: Electrification in Western Society, 1880–1930* (Baltimore: The Johns Hopkins Press, 1983). For the matters discussed here see especially Chapters 1 to 6.

15. On the shift in advertising style see T. J. Jackson Lears, "From Salvation to Self-Realization: Advertising and the Therapeutic Roots of the Consumer Culture, 1880–1930," in *The Culture of Consumption: Critical Essays in American History, 1880–1980*, Richard Wightman Fox and T.J. Jackson Lears, eds. (New York: Pantheon Books, 1983), pp. 1–38, and Michael McMahon "An American Courtship: Psychologists and Advertising Theory," *American Studies*, Vol. 13 (1972), pp. 5–18. For the most complete study to date of the "new" advertising style, see Roland Marchand, *Advertising the American Dream; Making Way for Modernity, 1920–1940* (Berkeley: Univ. of California Press, 1985).

16. We should distinguish two types of negotiation. The type required for adult commitment rests on the conviction that the negotiating partners seek a single resolution to their problems. They are "in this thing together" and must seek a working consensus. By contrast, America's labor-management negotiations assume that each side tries to get what it can from the other. Trade-offs between two discrete parties substitute for a single consensus.

17. J. Robert Lifton is the foremost scholar writing about the psychic effects of living in the nuclear age. See *Indefensible Weapons: The Political and Psychological Case Against Nuclearism,* with Robert Falk (New York: Basic Books, 1982).

18. Mk 16:16. In his interpretation of Vatican II, Karl Rahner, S.J. indicates one of the challenges for a shrinking world. He argues that the council inaugurated the third major epoch of the church. Jewish Christianity (first epoch) opened out into the church of "Hellenism and of European culture and civilization." Vatican II begins "the period in which the sphere of the church's life is in fact the entire world." Karl Rahner, S.J., "Towards a Fundamental Theological Interpretation of Vatican II," *Theological Studies* 40 (December 1979), p. 721.

Rahner does not discuss the post-World War II context of the council. I suggest here that the cumulative effect of western technological style in the past century should not be viewed, despite its frightening dimensions, as if it falls outside the workings of the Holy Spirit. From this perspective Vatican II might be understood as an early sign of the Holy Spirit working in us toward the redemption of our present situation.

Part Three

Perspectives on the Decline of Vocations

A Biblical Perspective on Why They Left

Donald Senior, C.P.

My reflections on the departures of American men and women religious in the past few decades will be from a "biblical" perspective since my field is scripture, with the hope that it might add something to the mix, even though the thrust of the reports is more properly sociological and psychological.

I write this immediately after returning from three months of teaching in Jerusalem. Mulling over the issues and reading the reports on the data while in that living laboratory of human history, far from the cultural context of the United States, gives a certain perspective. There people have long memories and history has to be viewed in terms of centuries and eras rather than decades. That leads me to think that trying to answer the questions of why people left religious life in such numbers and why too few candidates are entering must be put in the context of the enormous cultural changes that the western world (especially America) has experienced in the decades following World War II, particularly in the 1960s and 1970s.

As those who have reflected on the studies comment, the present situation of religious life cannot be reduced to any combination of moral factors (infidelity, weakness, lack of commitment, etc.). I cannot be persuaded that the state of religious life in the mid-twentieth century was any worse than in previous generations; in fact, one might make a case that it was much more vigorous than in many previous eras. The only thing that can explain the departure of tens of thousands of religious men and women in such a short period of time is an enormous cultural shift with its concomitant crisis of meaning.

In fact one could say that practically *everyone* left religious life during this time. Even most of those who "stayed" changed their way of being a religious in such a radical way as to have "left" the religious life they had originally joined. To search for some particular strain of "failure" in the quality of religious life as the cause of our problems or to hope that reassembling what we had before the explosion will bring any solution is, in my opinion, doomed to complete frustration.

I would like to put the psychological, sociological and theological aspects of that cultural revolution, as treated in the other essays, into a biblical framework.

It is possible to read the entirety of biblical history as an ongoing struggle of Israel and the early Christian community to discover there its religious identity and to remain faithful to it in the midst of an evolving cultural context.[1] The earliest generations of Israel were not immune to their cultural context, even though their theology stressed a God-given distinctiveness from the surrounding peoples. Israel's language, art forms, political structures, and even much of its religious thought and expression were adapted from Canaanite and other semitic cultures. Israel experienced profound enculturation in every aspect of its national and religious life. If it had not done so it would have died. In fact, much of the Bible is taken up with the struggle of the Jews to discern what elements of their evolving cultural context were compatible with their religious vision and which were alien or harmful to it.

In the two centuries before the birth of Christ, the major issue of the biblical writings (e.g. Daniel, Maccabees, etc.) was how Judaism should react to the incursions of Hellenistic culture, a culture that inexorably made its mark on Jewish life and faith, despite sectarian impulses that attempted to insulate people from it (e.g. the reforms of Ezra and Nehemiah).

One can view the entire New Testament from this perspective as well. The ministry of Jesus and the earliest post-resurrection community was played out in a Palestinian context. This milieu had been profoundly influenced by Hellenism but it was still quite different from the cultural arena of the "diaspora" in Greece, Rome or Alexandria. The inherently universal thrust of the gospel made it an imperative for early Christianity to cross cultural boundaries and to proclaim its message outside of a Palestinian Jewish context. Obviously this earliest Christian mission had enormous success. But it also caused profound transformations in the church's theology, structures and outlook.[2] Almost all of the New Testament writings were produced in response to the tensions and opportunities created by the enormous cultural transition the church was experiencing. In less than a century after the death and resurrection of Jesus, Christianity became thoroughly enculturated in the Greco-Roman world.

In a perceptive and now often-quoted article, Karl Rahner compared the cataclysmic changes signaled by the council to those experienced by early Jewish Christianity as it moved into the Greco-Roman milieu.[3] Beneath the surface issues of the council (e.g. vernacular in the liturgy, styles of authority, religious freedom, etc.) stood a much more basic and far-reaching issue: for the first time in its history the church was beginning to experience itself as a world church. The center of the church was beginning to feel the impact of non-European cultures, and the hegemony of Greco-Roman/ or European/western patterns of thought and meaning was being challenged for the first time in almost two thousand years of history.

I believe Rahner's intuition is essentially correct and has important implications for understanding the crisis of religious life in the United States in the period subsequent to the council. While enculturation is often discussed in relation to non-western culture, there has, until very recently, been little reflection on enculturation into *American* culture. It may have been assumed that European institutions (i.e. most forms of religious life) could continue to be absorbed into the American cultural stream with little or no adaptation. But when American culture itself has undergone serious convulsions—politically, educationally, socially—it is not surprising that American religious would subject their own religious subculture to severe and, at times, traumatic scrutiny.

Viewed from a general biblical perspective such transformations are inevitable. Viewed more specifically from a gospel perspective, the trauma of enculturation is a necessary by-product of the universality of the Christian message. The gospel must continually be "translated" into each human culture; otherwise it is culturally bound and not truly universal. Religious life, as an attempt to incarnate the gospel, cannot itself be immune from this demand.

From my perspective this is what is going on not only in religious life but in the church in general. The core intuition of Vatican II, expressed in numerous ways in its various documents, was the need for the church to renew its mission in the world. *Gaudium et Spes,* one of the last documents to be drafted and one that in the view of many observers best expressed the emerging spirit of the council, directly addressed the issue of the church's relation to the world and asserted the need for church to learn from, to be in vital contact with, as well as to be prophetically challenging to, secular reality. Perhaps only now, in the absence of euphoria and with the reactionary pull to return to old ways, is the church learning what a difficult task such a mission is.

The American Experience

Very little theological reflection has been done on the American experience of church.[4] This is a serious lack that needs a quick remedy. However it does not take a crystal ball to see some valid correlation between the recent transformations in religious life and key values of American culture. Many people have left and continue to leave religious life because of an as yet unresolved lack of connection between these two systems.

Allow me to list some typical and positive values of contemporary American culture. I am not claiming that these qualities are unique to the American experience or that they do not have negative aspects to them. Nor are they listed in a spirit of uncritical self-congratulation (which seems a bit epidemic in our country today). But assuming that every human culture has positive as well as negative values, it is important for us to be in touch with the wisdom of our own way of life. Some of these positive values of contemporary American culture would include the following:

1. Personalism. A strong emphasis of recent American culture is on "personal fulfillment." Individual talents and aspirations are considered worthy of encouragement. A high value is given to individual achievement and success. A style of religious life that stressed uniformity and suppression of self-expression was bound at some point to run against this strong cultural current.

Under this heading could also be placed the concern with interpersonal relationships as important to personal fulfillment. In a religious context this translates into a concern for authentic community, free from unnecessary formalism, an aspiration repeatedly expressed by new candidates for religious life. It is also linked to problems experienced in balancing friendship, intimacy and celibacy.

The emergence of feminist consciousness, while now no longer an exclusively North American phenomenon, is predictably American. It is not surprising that ecclesiastical authority shaped by a very different cultural experience finds the assertiveness of many American women religious threatening. Instead of reading it as an authenic expression of personhood it is often interpreted as insubordination.

2. Freedom and self-determination. This value is at the core of the American experience. Reaction to arbitrary use of authority inaugurated the American revolution and has remained, at least in principle, its guiding spirit. Is it surprising that perceived abuses of authority have been and remain a primary cause of disillusionment with religious and ecclesiastical life?

3. Pluralism. One of the most valuable aspects of the American cultural experience may be its inherently pluralistic character. Its major political institutions rest on the ability to form coalitions and to balance various groups and aspirations without suppressing diversity. Forms of religious life often shaped in a monarchical or aristocratic political milieu in which conformity and docility were prime values were bound at some point to clash with the American experience.

4. Democratic self-criticism. It would be foolhardy to claim that Americans are more effectively self-critical than any other culture or national group. Yet inherent to our political and social life are structures of self-criticism: a democratic form of government, a vigorous free press, autonomous educational systems, etc. Even if it is not exercised with uniform wisdom, the ability to dissent and critique are important American cultural and political assumptions. This, too, is a place where structures of religious and ecclesiastical life that gave very low value to dissent and democratic involvement in policy making were bound to clash with American culture.

5. Egalitarianism. Here is another important value in the American cultural mythology. In the United States the era of the Vatican Council was preceded by a revolutionary struggle of blacks for civil rights. Their claim on legal parity was based directly on the American dream (which, by the way, explicitly drew on a biblical basis) that all citizens, of whatever race,

color, creed, or gender, are created equal. The later emergence of feminism is, in many ways, a logical follow-through on this civil rights struggle. Again, could structures of religious life predicated on an essentially hierarchical view of society avoid, at some point, dissonance with this cultural value?

6. An emphasis on productivity and success. The American mythology also places a high value on work and job satisfaction. Esteem within the culture is often tied to success in the workplace. While religious life traditions have also placed a high value on work, the rapid change in theology and ecclesiology after the council left many religious "beached," unable to adapt to changing needs and therefore underemployed. This remains a critical problem in both men and women religious communities. Given the tendency of the culture to measure self-worth by productivity standards it is no wonder that underemployment contributes to the crisis of religious life in this country.

I would contend, therefore, that most of the problems experienced by religious orders in the wake of the council were part of a much broader and deeper process at work in American society. Prior to World War II American Catholicism was still a strongly sectarian phenomenon. Religious life was one piece of a Catholic ethos that carried its own cogency and was largely insulated from the currents of American culture. In the wake of World War II America enjoyed widespread economic prosperity. This led in turn to a whole new generation of citizens who no longer had to be absorbed in the struggle for subsistence but had the means for education and some leisure. At the same time American Catholicism became more self-confident, no longer an immigrant church, its members achieving economic, social and political parity with other Americans. Later the trauma and self-doubt of the Vietnam era led, in turn, to a searching review of American culture and institutions. All of this (and many other complicating factors) influenced religious life in America, too. The council itself was both a by-product of and a contributor to a self-conscious appraisal of western cultures. In this spirit religious communities were explicitly asked to review their founding impulse and to adapt it to the circumstances of modern life. Whatever multiple factors may be cited as contributing to the changes experienced by religious communities, it must not be forgotten that the principal cause is precisely the need to adapt the structures of religious life to a new and swiftly developing cultural situation. Even if they may not have expressly reflected on it previously, given the opportunity and even the mandate to adapt their structures to their contemporary world, the vast majority of American religious quickly realized the need for radical change. It is hard otherwise to explain how thousands of sincere men and women could have, practically overnight, shed religious practices they had performed faithfully for many years. Many could not find sufficient meaning or emotional support within the context of religious life and therefore left. Many others—probably the majority—made sweeping changes in their conception and practice of religious life. Very few continued business as usual. And even fewer religious, even if they are dissatisfied with their present lot, are tempted to return to the practices of former years. In the face of such widespread change I can only conclude that many of the structures of religious life were in strong dissonance with the surrounding culture. In history it has rarely been the church that sets the agenda for change; it is the larger forces of history and culture that force their agenda upon the church.

The biblical world has always known this. It is in the arena of history—and not simply in the confines of the temple—that God has worked the most sweeping changes. And that has been the case here, too. I dare to say that if the vast majority of religious prior to the 1960s were guaranteed to be faithful, studious, prayerful people, the gigantic changes charted in the sociological studies at our disposal would still have taken place.

By relating this profound transformation to the biblical drama, I am suggesting that this cultural adaptation is not a necessary evil but an imperative of the gospel. By relating the problems of religious life to the universal thrust of the gospel I am not, I hope, falling prey to romanticism or suggesting that all of the departures and problems of the past two decades were due only to noble efforts at adapting religious life to American culture. But perhaps for too long in this country religious life, and the church itself, retained an essentially European character.

It is also self-evident that adapting religious life to a contemporary culture does not mean wholesale acceptance of that culture's values and assumptions. American life is plagued with problems that are the shadow side of its positive values. But only to the degree that religious life has thoroughly adapted to American culture is it in a position to take a prophetic stance on American issues. The role of the prophet in a given society can never be adequately carried out by an "outsider"; only one who knows the traditions and the language of a culture can prophetically challenge it.

Conclusions: Why They Left and Why They Don't Come

In conclusion I would agree that the reasons for the massive departures from religious life in this country are multiple. But I would also contend that transcending the various presenting causes is the deeper issue of enculturation. In a period of profound cultural change and self-reflection, many religious were unable to retain an adequate rationale for their lives as consecrated religious. Many of them therefore left. Others chose not to leave but are part of an ongoing effort to adapt religious life to contemporary culture, with varying degrees of success. The process is not over and it seems unrealistic to attempt closure so soon. People continue to leave religious life (even if at a slower rate), and religious communities still struggle to find a deeper way of renewing their lives and structures. The process has become even more complex in the face of a reactionary mood now present in the church and society at large. (As Mark Twain wryly noted: People write poems about the trees when the railroad is about to come through.)

The continued struggle of religious life in this country to adapt to modern American culture is, in my view, the single most important reason for the small number of candidates. In my experience, many of the young people who apply for religious life are seeking support and security in a turbulent world. Obviously a religious community that is itself part of that turbulence is not going to be an attractive option. And other potential candidates capable of living with uncertainty, and anxious to do something significant, do not think of religious life as a relevant way of being involved and, accurately or not, view religious as out of touch with modern life.

As many others have commented, there is not really a decline in "vocations" in our country. Increasing numbers of lay people who formerly would have entered religious communities now look elsewhere. In my experience, the forms of Christian life they long for often correspond with the positive values of American society outlined above. Many women, in particular, shy away from religious life because they fear it is shackled by an unsympathetic church authority; therefore significant numbers seek a religious way of life in other quarters, even to the point of leaving the Roman Catholic communion. Therefore I would suggest that the ultimate remedy to the "vocation crisis" is not to slow, much less to reverse, the process of adaptation but for religious to continue it and for ecclesiastical authority to publicly support it.

I suspect that before the Spirit of God has completed the

work of bringing the gospel into deep contact with our culture, many of the existing forms of religious life will wither and die. They served a noble purpose and enabled thousands of good Christians to lead authentic evangelical lives. It is not a tragedy that they should have served their purpose and pass on; it has happened time and time again in the long history of Christianity. At the same time, I believe that radical forms of monastic and contemplative religious life will flourish and be an important source of theological reflection and ecumenism (among Christian bodies and with other religious traditions). And when enough dying has taken place in the old forms, renewed communities of active, celibate religious will also be on the scene. Undoubtedly these will be smaller in number than previously but more in tune with the symbols and structures of the modern world and therefore freer to be important witnesses to authentic Christian life and vital components in the church's global ministry.

Notes

1. A detailed illustration of this in both Old and New Testaments is made in D. Senior and C. Stuhlmueller, *The Biblical Foundations for Mission* (Maryknoll: Orbis, 1983).

2. See, for example, R. Brown, *The Churches the Apostles Left Behind* (New York: Paulist Press, 1984).

3. Karl Rahner, "Towards a Fundamental Theological Interpretation of Vatican II," *Theological Studies* 40 (1979) 716–727.

4. Some work groups are now attempting to formulate a North American theology; see, for example, D. Flaherty (ed.), *Working Papers . . . Toward a North American Theology* (Chicago: Center for Pastoral Ministry, 1981), and T. O'Connell (ed.), *Vatican II and Its Documents* (Wilmington: Michael Glazier, 1986).

Biblical Observations on the Decline of Vocations to Religious Life

Carroll Stuhlmueller, C.P.

From my background in biblical studies, especially in Old Testament prophecy, and from personal experience, I am led to seven areas of investigation for the decline in religious vocations today. The first three items reflect the sociological changes in the United States, the next three spring from a biblical setting, and the final section centers on unresolved theological questions.

The Changing Forms of the Apostolate

The forms of the apostolate have been changing during the last twenty years. Until Vatican II, women religious dedicated their lives and their abilities to the American church almost exclusively in one of two apostolates—as teachers or in health care. But the dismantling of many parochial schools was under way even before Vatican II, or, at the least, confidence in their future was eroding. Certainly there were doubts about their role for the very poor, who were being priced out of many parochial schools. As a result some women religious began to direct their sights to other forms of the apostolate, not only in parish ministry, but often outside parish boundaries through service as chaplains in jails and hospitals, or in campus ministries.

Religious women began to live alone because their work was often geographically separate from convents of their own order, or because of the hours and specific nature of their work. They became financially responsible within a fixed budget and managed their own funds. In some ways their ministry began to resemble that of diocesan priests.

In considering these changes in the apostolate, one must remember that members of women's communities do not have the choice, as most men's communities provide, between the lay vocation of a brother and the priestly, ordained vocation. Men religious have continued to keep in closer touch with the parochial and sacramental ministry of the church, with the bishops who grant faculties for these ministries, and with the theology of the church. Men religious, all along, have shown greater diversity in ministry and lifestyle, have shared in the stability of the larger church (and usually in the latter's financial resources), and generally have been able to count on a more consistent theological training, at least before ordination. Women religious, however, have tended to take better advantage of continuing education after their profession of vows.

If we are to attract vocations to women's communities, it may be necessary to arrive at new legislation that clarifies and more accurately reflects their living situation. Perhaps women should be given the opportunity to form associations more similar to the diocesan priesthood—associations which envision living alone, having responsibility for one's own funds, receiving trust and support in their work, health insurance, etc. Their new forms of the apostolate will reach at times beyond individual parishes or dioceses—like the movements for peace and a just economy and, for example, soup kitchens and pantries, shelters for homeless people, and training of liturgical ministers. Or the sisters might be placed in charge of parishes or specific ministries within the parish, directly under the bishops as diocesan priests are.

The canonical procedure of the church needs to reach out to many new forms of ministry. Clear job descriptions will be necessary, not only for security but also to ensure justice. This suggestion presupposes that the church will provide financial assistance in education for ministry, good placement in employment with adequate compensation, and "fringe benefits" that will include health insurance, pensions, and a mandate from the bishop with his support and affirmation. No matter what one's motives are for a religious vocation, serious financial burdens and insecure tenure with jobs will deter applicants.

As women religious push out in new directions, young women may once again be attracted to a life strong in its continuity and vibrant with hope—if these new directions can be clarified and helped by episcopal support. Unless the bishops give this support, women religious will too often be viewed with suspicion by the laity and with fear by the priests.

In my contact with Protestant seminaries and their students, I have been amazed at the growing number of Roman Catholics in their student bodies, and particularly Catholics who come from minority groups—women, blacks and Hispanics. (I include women here as a minority group, for their number is small compared to men in theological and pastoral training centers of the Catholic Church.) Minority groups are going to the Protestant seminaries because of good scholarship money and because of a warm student body and a faculty which includes a sizable number of people from minority groups. They find their "language" spoken more spontaneously and more continuously.

To my knowledge, no adequate questionnaire has been devised and used to assess the role of women in Roman Catholic seminaries and schools of theology. In my experience, women and lay students have come to the seminary with a significant pastoral experience, and know exactly where they need and want updating. Money for their study is carefully budgeted. They not only make the best use of their time, but they are generally in the higher bracket of student achievement and so contribute in an important way to the tone of the classroom.

While some of them are desirous of ordination to priesthood, the opportunity to prepare for parish and other types of religious ministry is satisfying and tends to defuse the ordination question. Today there is seldom if ever any public demonstration as there once was.

Change in Social Status and Service Roles

Previously, religious life or priesthood was a means by which the individual religious, as well as his or her family, acquired a higher social and religious status. In families where there were many children, it was beneficial if one or even several entered religious life and the priesthood.

For women especially, but also for men, a religious vocation was almost the only way to offer one's services for humanitarian purposes or for religious work. This is no longer the case in the United States, so that an incentive for vocations that was important in the past is no longer present. In the past some religious, perhaps many, joined their congregation as the only means for them to engage in humanitarian or religious roles of service. After Vatican II new possibilities of service opened up within the church and outside it. Some have left the religious life in order to continue their original vocation, which was not to religious life but to humanitarian service.

The Lay Apostolate

There is a need to accentuate the lay apostolate—the seedbed of vocations to religious life and to priesthood. This is especially the case with members of minority groups who presently have great difficulties surviving in our seminaries and religious houses. It has been pointed out in the Neal and CARA reports that young people are fearful of lifelong commitments. Perhaps if they are given a taste of the apostolate in a temporary way, they will be drawn to the work for their term of life. Given proper training with diocesan and religious seminarians, more of these lay people may well choose the joy of a lifelong celibate vocation for themselves. In other words, if religious life is to be reformed so that it will be more attractive to new recruits, this reformation cannot be done in isolation from reform in other ministerial offices within the church, including seminaries. If these latter are turned back into exclusively priesthood centers, religious vocations will be negatively affected and the quality of training will suffer. The new priests will tend to think of themselves as uniquely different and superior, and as a result will not properly respect the talents and responsibilities of non-ordained persons.

We must also look realistically at other reasons for the lack of vocations among blacks and Hispanics. For example, Hispanics, once they enter the seminary, often find that their education is almost exclusively in Anglo suburban areas, and come to feel that they are being separated too long from their own people and culture. As a result, they may find that they end up with more theological knowledge, but less pastoral effectiveness. There is an unusually strong urgency to prepare priests and other ministers quickly for the Hispanic communities, and these communities cannot wait for qualified applicants to spend *long* years in college and theological studies, whether for priesthood or for other forms of ministry.

Prayer and Bible Study

Focus on prayer and Bible study is the least developed area in the CARA/Neal reports. Nevertheless, there has been significant development among both men and women religious in such movements as houses of prayer, thirty-day retreats, prayer groups, courses in spirituality, and the preparation of spiritual directors. Religious women particularly have emphasized this side of their life. This new affirmation of prayer may be a healthy reaction to the stress upon social action and political involvement among religious. A public affirmation of prayer and Bible study by church authority cannot hurt vocations and recruitment!

Bible study inevitably leads to an enthusiastic desire to share the new learning. It imparts a new maturity and independence in religious and moral matters, and whets the appetite for religious ministry. This is one reason why Bible enthusiasts among the laity and among religious gravitate toward Protestant churches, especially the non-sacramental types, where they can be quickly endorsed as ministers of religion. These same people might well remain loyal Catholics if they were given the opportunity to have ministerial roles within the church. If priesthood is denied them because they are married or because they are female, they nonetheless are ready and prepared to conduct non-sacramental services.

From this background we can understand why Catholic charismatics do not have a good survival rate in our seminaries and religious houses. Their association with non-sacramental forms of devotion (often enough forced upon them because the leaders of prayer groups are married or women and so cannot be ordained to the priesthood) induces a different setting for prayer than what they find in seminaries and religious houses. The quality and style of prayer are also very different from the more sacramental types of formal worship.

Bible study, therefore, has created its own strain of discontent among religious who are not priests and makes its own demands if recruitment is to be effective among this extremely talented group of young people.

Prophetic Mission and Vocations

Religious women, more so than men clerical religious, have undertaken a way of life closely attuned to Old Testament prophecy. Their religious style blends (a) that of the prophetic bands who centered around such individuals as Samuel (1 Sm 9–10) or around Elijah and Elisha (1 Kgs 17—2 Kgs 6), and (b) that of the classical prophets before the exile with books to their name (i.e. Amos, Hosea, Jeremiah). Especially when the modeling resembles the classical prophets, we ought not to expect many vocations. Instead, we find difficulties which strain the endurance even of the most stalwart of prophets or religious. Prophetic ministry, as the books of Hosea, Jeremiah and Isaiah reveal, is torn by agony, loneliness, at times a feeling of abandonment by God, and a long waiting without apparent success.

Prophecy is not an institution with clear identity and assured permanence. Prophecy, instead, has many "roles." Some prophets were leaders of worship, like Samuel and Ezekiel (1 Sm 9–10; Ez 14:1); others, like Amos, almost disdained this role within liturgy (Am 4:4–5). As in the days of Israel's prophets, forms of prophecy are evolving today, whether in social or racial questions, or in the arena of peace and economy. The tactics and associations that were effective only fifteen years ago are today often considered out of style and impotent.

Biblical prophecy ran into extreme difficulty with religious authorities, as we can see in the famous debate between the high priest Amaziah and the prophet Amos (Am 7:10–17) or between the prophet Jeremiah and the temple personnel (Jer 26).

Religious life, therefore, according to its prophetic modeling, ought not to expect many recruits. Prophets had but few disciples in their lifetime. And we should not be surprised at a heavy attrition rate, as happened to the prophet Jesus.

The prophetic role will leave its members burnt out, and therefore an easy prey to consolation from non-church sources. Whenever this happens today to religious, they find it very difficult to return to a church setting.

Community life is not very evident among the classical

prophets such as Amos, Hosea, Jeremiah and Ezekiel. Even the community around Jesus was very limited, homeless, and with little or no financial security.

This prophetic type of life and leadership depends for its existence upon a strong, heroic individual. Perhaps one of the most serious, inherent weaknesses of religious life today is that many of the heroic leaders are not properly and openly recognized by the church.

Another aspect of Old Testament prophetic ministry has strong parallels with the ministries of many religious women and men today. When prophets condemned the excessive formalism of liturgical worship or its cold indifference toward the suffering of the poor, they did so on what may seem humanitarian grounds: hunger, homelessness, unemployment, imprisonment, human indignities (i.e. Is 1; Mi 2–3). Prophets, however, are not motivated simply by humanitarian needs. They speak in the name of a compassionate and faithful God, as revealed to Moses at Sinai (Ex 34). For this reason they were reaching behind liturgical worship to its origins with Moses who liberated slaves out of Egypt in the name of God who declared: "I have witnessed the affliction of my people in Egypt and have heard their cry of complaint against their slave drivers" (Ex 3:7). Often enough in the past priests and other high religious officials have been unable to understand the issues. While prophets spoke from the agony of world needs, priests responded by invoking ritual laws and theological traditions. Prophetic vocations in almost every case led to severe strains between prophets and organizational leaders. We can observe similar tension and confusion today. The call to work prophetically within the church or within church-sponsored religious orders will enmesh religious in a web of ambiguity and conflict. Such conditions are not conducive to many vocations.

If we study the long and complex way by which the ministry of the prophets, their preaching and symbolic actions, came to be contained in a book under their names, we realize the necessity of *time*. It was not just decades but a century or more, for instance, before the preaching of Isaiah and his successors turned into the sixty-six chapters of the book of Isaiah. If religious in our contemporary church have turned in a strong prophetic direction, then the brief twenty to thirty years since Vatican II are hardly enough for their mission, charism and canonical structure to take a firm shape. The intention of the Vatican to finalize this experimental stage of religious updating runs against this prophetic model.

The difficulties and suffering, the disappointments and rejections of the prophetic ministry may explain why those religious who are engaged in it still remain at peace, yet do not encourage other young people to follow them. In sum, the extent to which religious life follows a prophetic model will be the extent to which it is reduced severely in numbers, the extent to which it is subjected to a high attrition rate.

Conservatism—Fundamentalism

The phenomenon of fundamentalism among young people, especially on college campuses, sheds light on their non-attraction to a religious vocation.

It is being recognized that fundamentalism is much more than a biblical problem; it may even be primarily a psychological and sociological situation. Fundamentalists are not necessarily sectarian or religious. They are found among (a) people reacting to great insecurities like poverty, addictions, world crises, preoccupation with future jobs; (b) people with relatively secure situations, with property and investments, who fear any unsettlement with the status quo; (c) people reacting to the sterile, overly scientific types of Bible study and to non-inspiring liturgies.

Any return among religious orders to what would be

interpreted as conservative fundamentalism needs to be carefully evaluated. Recruits from this background also ought to be screened. If they need a strict disciple or the perks and garbs of priesthood, their motivation may be more personal than what is generally good for church ministry and religious orders.

Theological Questions

There remain several serious questions which need to be investigated, their statement more carefully nuanced and their implications spelled out with more creativity. They are not closed doctrinal issues; they also impinge closely upon our discussion of perseverance in religious life and the recruitment of new applicants. Let me briefly discuss three of these issues.

(a) The nature of priesthood. Can we see new forms of expressing sacramental leadership in the church? Can we research into the possibility of ordaining a person for single specific ministries, like the anointing of the sick, the sacrament of reconciliation, or preaching? Would this be a way of contemplating the question of the ordination of women to sacramental ministry? An assurance from the pope and bishops that this question is being carefully scrutinized by accepted theologians, male and female, from the international community would greatly defuse the unrest over the question of ordination of women to priesthood.

According to the Neal report, only 1.8% of those surveyed thought that the "need for ordination of women" was one of the "main problems facing religious congregations today." Yet, the fact that this same report shows such a strong leaning away from "church" issues toward more secular forms of the apostolate ought to raise some alarm. The fact, furthermore, that more women religious and lay persons are conducting church services, without the eucharist or other sacramental action, indicates a decided drift toward Protestant forms of non-sacramental worship.

From the many roles already fulfilled by women religious in the apostolate of the Catholic Church in America, we ought to ascertain which ones are the most successful in leading people to a strong sense of justice and peace, to a firm commitment to prayer and forgiveness, to a renewed enthusiasm for being Catholic. The next step might associate these apostolic works with sacramental ministry.

(b) The question of sexuality has not been adequately addressed within the church. So long as a sizable number of the Catholic laity remain convinced that contraception is morally permissible under some circumstances, and so long as young people remain unconvinced of the official church position that sexual morality has no parvity of matter (so that a single act of masturbation is considered seriously sinful), there will be anger and suspicion toward church authority among a notable segment of the Catholic population. Mothers and fathers will be unwilling to recommend a religious vocation; young people will be still more hesitant about undertaking a difficult life of celibacy in an unresolved area of morality. I am not asking for quick solutions, but I am voicing my opinion that unless some study commissions are set up, composed of an international board of scholars freely nominated by the conferences of bishops in consultation with theological societies, and unless American Catholics know about it, sexuality will continue to be a serious barrier to recruitment.

(c) The Catholic Church, since 1960, has provided the wonderful experience of Vatican II, but since the council it has also had some very bad moments to live down. Reconciliation of the Vatican with religious will require some genuine ways of manifesting sorrow and of showing that the past tragedies will not happen again. An example is the way that the Immaculate Heart of Mary Sisters of Los Angeles were treated. Just by accident I happened to be at their college for some summer teaching in 1970 when all of them (with the single exception of Sister Dunstan, who was then over one hundred years old) were obliged to choose either to join a small group of less than fifty members (the remnant of a congregation once over six hundred members) or else to sign a document reducing them to the lay state. The wording was frigid and legal, with never a word of appreciation for these sisters' years of generous service. The older sisters felt trapped; all the chapter members and the former mother generals, along with the motherhouse with its infirmary, remained with the large body of the new group. Moreover, the Blessed Sacrament was to be removed from the chapel where the elderly sisters lived!

A more recent example is the way that the religious were treated who signed the ad in the *New York Times* about abortion. I am not defending the appropriateness or even the legitimacy of the ad. Some, however, who signed the ad never intended their names to appear publicly; others were responding over severe hurt, more in anger than according to a doctrinal stance. Yet the Vatican response was as harsh as could possibly be, and the sting was felt as much upon the major superiors as upon those who signed the document. Laity escaped unscathed. I know of several young people who would not want to be religious and subject themselves to such sudden recrimination without a hearing. And I know of lay people who left employment with Catholic publishing houses because of other abrupt forms of Vatican intervention. More examples can be cited, such as the way that the Discalced Carmelite nuns have been treated, and the Vatican reaction to liberation theologians. All of these actions are the cause of anger and frustration among religious men and religious women. It leaves them in a poor mood for encouraging vocations, and at times even for persevering themselves.

That something positive and public can be done is evident

from other good signs in the American church: the fact that religious women and brothers are serving as chancellors in some dioceses, and as pastoral administrators of some parishes; the bishops' style of conducting hearings, and the pastoral on women; the existence and the credibility already gained by the commission studying the decline in vocations to the religious life, headed by the archbishop of San Francisco, John R. Quinn.

Conclusion

The seven factors, touched upon in this chapter, come forward from insights into our contemporary church through biblical focus. If space had permitted, we would see that the shifting scene of church life and the new roles of men and women in society can be tracked as well in the Bible. Biblically new offices of leadership emerged. The highlighting of the lay apostolate is a natural setting for studying Old Testament prophecy. Its heroic demands help us to recognize the same courageous expectations today—and the resultant loss of the less stalwart and the decline in applicants. A fundamentalist answer with security and authority is hardly the right response. Finally, if religious change happened in biblical times, due to large political and sociological mutations, then several theological issues need to be investigated anew in our contemporary, shifting world—particularly the topics of priesthood and sexuality, two areas removed from serious scrutiny at Vatican II.

The Vocation Decline of Women Religious: Some Historical Perspectives

Mary Ewens, O.P.

Writing from the interdisciplinary viewpoint that characterizes my field of American studies, and conscious of the importance of women's history and the women's movement, I would like to examine some salient features of the whole history of sisters in America and the options that American women have had in different epochs. There are aspects of American culture, values, and customs that can help us to understand what has happened to American sisters in the last two decades. Scholars who have studied the post-Vatican II exodus from convents also have valuable insights to offer.

Eighteenth and Nineteenth Century Experiences

Alexis de Tocqueville's shrewd observations in *Democracy in America* on differences between American and European attitudes toward women point to several characteristics of women's roles that are germane to this essay. He notes that "in France women commonly received a reserved, retired, and almost conventual education, as they did in aristocratic times," but that in America they are taught to be independent, to think for themselves, to speak with freedom, and to act on their own impulses. They are given a knowledge of evil of all kinds, that they may learn to shun it. After marriage, however, he says that European women "have a great deal of freedom to carry on business and manage their own affairs, whereas American women become prisoners of their own house."[1] Many historians have documented the narrow confines of the lives of nineteenth century American women, and the struggles and resistance faced by those who tried to break out of that mold.

The lives of American nuns (I use the term in its broader, more popular meaning), however, were in sharp contrast with this description, despite the fact that they were hemmed in by cloistral regulations. It is evident from their writings and their histories that their lives were full of challenge, adventure, and excitement. For those who came from Europe, the romance of foreign travel and exotic experiences in a new land, with the exalted mission of spreading the gospel and doing the Lord's will, must have had tremendous appeal.

They endured severe hardships but worked together toward common goals, and there was plenty of scope for the development of individual talents. Often young women in their twenties were sent to distant regions to start new branches of their communities. Postulants and novices usually worked right along with the professed sisters and learned religious life by living it, under the watchful guidance of the older sisters. In times of war, sisters went off to nurse the wounded, or brought them into their own homes. When disaster struck, they were there to help.

One of the most interesting aspects of the lives of some of the sisters in the nineteenth century is the number of close friendships with men that they enjoyed. The priests who were their ecclesiastical superiors or chaplains often became their mentors, defenders, advisors, and friends. Their letters show that mutual friends shared common goals, performed services large and small for one another, sent gifts on special days, arranged little surprises, confided the deepest aspirations of their hearts, and prayed for one another.

Mother Seton had numerous friendships with men, including her benefactors, the Filicchi brothers, Archbishop John Carroll, and Fathers Pierre Babade and Simon Bruté.

Mother Theresa Gerhardinger confided to Father Mathias Siegert all of her problems, hopes, and fears. Bishop Bouvier of Le Mans was a friend to Mother Theodore Guerin, as were several American priests who stood by her in her altercations with her bishop. Mother Philippine Duchesne gained strength from her friendship with Fathers Barat and Varin. Providence Sister St. Francis Xavier's letters to Father Augustine Martin (later bishop of Natchitoches) were filled with remarks about their friendship, as when she wrote, "Friendship that has an end never had a beginning. Ours began in God; it continues in Him without any other tie than prayer; it therefore can never end."[2]

Let me underscore here some of the salient points about the lives of sisters in the eighteenth and nineteenth centuries. Their lives were in marked contrast to those of other women. Entrance into the convent provided a highly respectable way of life to young women who did not relish confinement in the roles of wife and mother. It was one of the few careers open to those who wanted to serve the church and the broader human family. The number of sisters in America increased from just under 1,500 in 1850 to around 40,000 by 1900. Though there are many factors involved in this increase, including immigration from Europe, this aspect of an alternate career outside of marriage must have had something to do with it. The contrast with the situation today is obvious.

Despite the restrictions of cloister, in most sisters' lives there was a great deal of interaction with the people they served, including friendships with men, a mix of new recruits with professed sisters, and a great deal of travel from mission to mission, as well as involvement with new missions, new buildings, and new projects as the church and the country grew and prospered. Half the students in a school might be Protestant, and boarding students often lived within convent precincts. Was there a warmer family spirit and more genuine affection in the convents of that period? Who can tell? But life seems to have been simpler, less hemmed in with petty regulations, and more wholesome than it was in some convents in a later period.

Europeanization of American Religious Life

Sisters who came to America from convents in Europe soon learned that adaptation of their European customs to the very different culture of America was one of the greatest challenges they faced. They may not have *liked* what they saw of American ways but they had to make some concessions if their works were to succeed. No one doubted that there were differences; the letters of European sisters are full of descriptions of American traits and values.

In the last decades of the nineteenth century, many congregations of sisters sought Vatican approval of their constitutions. Often they were advised by those who "knew the ropes" in Rome to adopt constitutions from communities which had already been approved by the Vatican so as to facilitate the process. In so doing, they also took on customs from European cultures that were entirely foreign to their own traditions. In some instances, particularly at first, when many objected to the imposition of strange customs, superiors held certain parts of these constitutions in abeyance. Later superiors might have forgotten—if they ever knew—what the original spirit of the congregation was like, and why regulations that did not fit that spirit had been included in their constitutions. Little attention was paid, when it came to approving constitutions, to the differences that all astute commentators had seen between American and European women in manners, training and roles.

Thus a basic tension developed between the prescriptions of constitutions and the authentic spirit of a congregation.

Customs which made a community "fit into" the local scene and the families among whom its members worked and from whom new recruits came might now be abrogated. Problems were heightened when prescriptions from Roman law were interpreted with an English common law mentality.

Italian churchmen whose observation of nineteenth century European history made them highly suspicious of all democratic tendencies fought to keep American values from seeping into the western European cultural ambiance that marked the "Catholic" Church. In the last decade of the nineteenth century they tried to stamp out the "phantom heresy" of Americanism. A misinterpretation of the efforts of the Paulists to meet the needs of the contemporary American church was the cause of the tempest. The encyclical *Testem Benevolentiae*, which Pope Leo XIII addressed to Cardinal Gibbons in 1899, reflects a certain attitude toward the modernization and Americanization of traditional practices which should be noted. American ideas were suspect then in Rome and, I contend, are still suspect now.

Twentieth Century Developments

In the early part of the twentieth century, with the termination of the missionary status of America in 1908, the codification of canon law in 1917, and the growth and institutionalization of religious communities, a different spirit developed among them. An understanding of what happened after 1917 is essential, I think, if one hopes to comprehend what happened to religious communities of women in the 1960s.

The codification of canon law resulted in the promulgation of cloistral regulations for nuns which dated back to medieval times, when unwilling nuns were sometimes consigned to convents by their parents and had to be kept there by force. All contact with the outside world was carefully controlled, and was looked upon as a snare of the devil which might distract a sister from the pure contemplation of God. This may have been salutary when almost all nuns were cloistered contemplatives, but it put sisters at a distinct disadvantage when they were expected to prepare their students to grapple with the real world of the twentieth century.

This separation from the world was emphasized in the novitiate, where the new recruit was initiated into the behavior patterns that would be expected of her. Novices no longer became a part of a convent endeavor such as a school or a hospital, where they could learn "on the job" the essentials of religious life, as they had in the nineteenth century. Now they had an intensive training period during which they were separated not only from their families and previous associates, but also from the other members of the community which they were joining. While the essentials of the religious life remained the same, an emphasis on the letter of the law and on external details of behavior sometimes obscured the spirit of the gospels which was the basic motivating force.

Sociologists who have studied "total institutions," which aim at total control of a person's life and inculcation of new values and ideologies as well as new lifestyles, have found that methods of gaining this kind of control are similar in prisons, mental institutions, concentration camps, cults, and convents. Erving Goffman's *Asylums* is instructive on this point. Helen Ebaugh was a nun when she began a sociological study of former nuns. She had left her community by the time she came to write her book *Out of the Cloister*. In it she describes data collected from questionnaires sent to hundreds of congregations, and interviews with nineteen former members from each of three communities, one "liberal," one "conservative," and one "middle of the road." Ebaugh discusses Robert Lifton's *Thought Reform and the Psychology of Totalism* at some length.[3] Lifton studied brainwashing techniques used to get Chinese prisoners to take on the goals and attitudes of the

Communist Party. Much of what he found is similar to what was done in novitiates.

A process of death and rebirth was basic to the method. It involved death unto oneself, a negation of natural impulses, an emptying of all that is not pure. Social control is achieved in several ways. Milieu control is crucial; it ensures control of human communication—not only all external information and exchange but even what enters the mind. Relations between the self and the outer world—which usually help us to validate our self-concept—are disrupted. Ebaugh describes what this involves:

> The person is deprived of the combination of external information and internal reflection which anyone requires to test the realities of her environment and maintain a measure of identity separate from it. Rather, the individual is called upon to make an absolute polarization of the "real," that is, the prevailing ideology, and the "unreal," that is, everything else (p. 41).

Among the techniques used are a demand for purity which increases one's sense of shame and guilt, confession of faults to relieve guilt, and the primacy of doctrine over person, dogma over experience. Ebaugh parallels all of Lifton's findings with the actual practice in convents.

Brainwashing, thought control and conditioning are not techniques that we want to apply to religious life, but the evidence that similar practices were used in novitiates is rather powerful. Elements of "deprogramming" came in when sisters were exposed to new people, ideologies, and lifestyles as a result of education and renewal. There is a basic similarity among the experiences of all American sisters up to the time of the Second Vatican Council, even though individual communities, because of their traditions or the basic good sense of superiors, may have interpreted canon law with more latitude than did others.

The wind which blew in the fresh air of the Second Vatican Council actually began as a gentle breeze in 1939, when Pope Pius XII began to address women regarding their obligation to "work for the improvement of society" through civic and political action.

Pius XII probably did not realize the far-reaching results of his remarks to the International Congress of Major Superiors in 1952 when he said:

> In the training of your sisters for the tasks that await them, be broadminded and liberal and admit of no stinginess. Whether it be for teaching, the care of the sick, the study of art or anything else, the sister should be able to say to herself, "My superior is giving me a training that will put me on an equality with my secular colleagues." Give them also the opportunity and the means to keep their professional knowledge up-to-date. This is important for your sisters' peace and for their work.[4]

The Sister Formation Movement grew out of that conference. This movement emphasized the importance of adequate professional education for sisters before they went out to teach or nurse. It burgeoned in the 1950s, when schools were beginning to bulge with the children of the post-war baby boom generation. To send young sisters off to college just when they were so badly needed in the Catholic schools was difficult, but many communities managed somehow to do it.

Ebaugh is right, I think, when she writes, "The Sister Formation Movement had unanticipated consequences for religious orders, consequences that were so great and touched such vital areas of religious orders that history might well show that the Sister Formation Movement marked the beginning of the fragmentation of religious orders in the United States."[5]

Autobiographical Accounts

This is an age of story-telling, and it is my feeling that stories of the experiences of individual sisters who left can give flesh and human feeling to the cold statistical data of reports.

In the Neal study, community administrators reported that sisters left their congregations because of a lack of personal fulfillment, dissatisfaction with community life, and a preference for marriage, among other reasons. Perhaps we can get at the reasons *behind* these reasons, and come to a better understanding of the exodus, if we look at some actual experiences of a few of the sisters who left.

Autobiographical writings of twentieth century nuns, as well as former nuns, include long descriptions of the novitiate experience and the new way of life that it taught: the rules of "religious decorum" and silence, the daily horarium, the religious garb, prayer, and the vows. The young sister had to master what was virtually a whole new culture, with its own vocabulary and customs, including such minute details of behavior as the proper way to eat a banana or crush the shell after having consumed an egg. These books always include stories of the catastrophes that can assail novices or postulants who apply their former "worldly" standards of judgment in new situations in which they are no longer appropriate.

Their descriptions of the lives of professed nuns reveal that while twentieth century sisters still enjoyed educational and occupational opportunities, and administered their own institutions, there was far less healthy contact with lay adults and one's own family in this century. Superiors continued to be involved in decision-making at all levels, but the individual sister was not, and we no longer saw young women in their early twenties setting out to conquer the world, unless they were in the foreign missions. Most sisters lived in a world restricted to children and to other nuns. Many were forbidden to read newspapers, listen to the radio, or watch television, and there was much less awareness of, or participation in, the world outside the parish or hospital. Fortunately there is evidence that common sense and a creative spirit enabled many to lead rich, full lives despite the restrictions of canon law.

Let us now turn to the writings of some of the sisters who left the religious life during this period. Mary McCarran, daughter of Senator Pat McCarran, entered the Convent of the Holy Names in 1925, and left it thirty-two years later when her widowed mother required her assistance. In her autobiography she describes her novitiate experience in great detail: learning the proper way to walk, performing penances, keeping her eyes cast down, giving up her own individuality and taking on "the community mold." She tells of the rules that prescribed one change of underwear and two baths per week, the confiscation of letters from men, restrictions on her contacts with college friends, and a reprimand for laughing at a joke in chapel.

Even more disturbing than her novitiate stories are those of her first years on mission, when the inane conversations and restrictions on newspapers and on walking outside made her feel "like a caged prisoner." Nor did she experience the sisterhood that is so evident in the writings of many nineteenth century nuns: "I slept in the same room with Sister Rosemary for one year, and I don't believe there was ever a night that I did not cry myself to sleep. Not once during that time did she ever ask if there was anything she could do to help me." When she found a helpful spiritual advisor, and a close friendship developed between them, neither she, nor her superiors, nor the priest himself was able to cope with the situation. It was her father who finally solved the dilemma of this "particular friendship." Senator Pat McCarran had expressed his anger over the rigidity of convent life early in the game and had tried to persuade Mary to come home, but she stayed for another thirty years before following his advice. After her father's death, when convent rules kept her from helping her mother with her business affairs, Sister Mary Mercy left her community.[6]

No book better conveys the tensions, hopes, fears, and realities of the period after the council than Mary Griffin's *The Courage To Choose*. Particularly valuable are her analysis of the system by which she was trained in the novitiate, and her explanation of the reasons for the changes enacted after Vatican II. Griffin's memories of the "incarceration" of her novitiate days are as negative as those of Mary McCarran. The most destructive aspect of the experience for her was the emphasis on the evil of "particular friendships," which, in the interpretation of some, "placed all friendship strictly out of bounds for the rest of their lives."[7] She wrote: "The horror of religious life was not, I realized sadly, what its detractors, writing in the tradition of Maria Monk or *The Devils of Loudon*, took to be the dark underside of the convent. It was the emptiness, the hollowness of a life devoid of human love—however dedicated to God." And, reflecting back on the whole experience of the postulancy: "As I look back now, I observe in myself and in my companions a noticeable regression during the postulancy. Day after day we were urged to work for humility, dependence, the simplicity of a child, and to try to be to our superiors as 'limpid water in a crystal vase.' The result was often a kind of infantilism and a resurgence of childhood needs for reassurance, security, affection—rewards for being good 'children,' striving for self-abnegation, discipline, self-surrender to God."

Mary Griffin traces the stages in her own consciousness-raising from marching at Selma to teaching at a college for blacks in Mississippi and participating in demonstrations against the Vietnam War—and the process whereby her community reexamined its role in the contemporary world and implemented sweeping changes in the lives of its members.

Why did she leave her community? Her answer is similar to those which Ebaugh finds to be typical of those liberal congregations which responded very quickly to the decrees of Vatican II:

> Mainly [I left] because I had come to realize that I had grown into quite another person from the twenty-two-year-old girl who once felt compelled to "follow a vocation" and dedicate myself to Catholic education. Today I am convinced that God has really no plan for me other than the one I evolve for myself. Since I feel able to grow more fully as a person outside the structure of religious life, then that is His will for me (p. 200).

In her book, *Nun: A Memoir*, Mary Gilligan Wong recounts episodes of eleven years in a religious community, and weaves into the tale the experiences of more than forty other former nuns whom she has interviewed, many of them from her congregation. The facts that she entered the novitiate just before the start of the Second Vatican Council and participated in the early phases of renewal, and that she is now a clinical psychologist, make her account extremely useful.[8]

Wong's generation was the last to experience an "old style" novitiate. She describes the censorship of mail, dressing under her nightgown, being told to control her emotions, and the constant striving for humility, self-abnegation, and child-like dependence on superiors.

She was inspired by her reading of Cardinal Suenens' ground-breaking book, *The Nun in the World:*

Hearing his ideas about how nuns should not be so cloistered excites and liberates us, and we hang on every bold word . . . we begin to see the world as the vineyard where we will labor, not as a treacherous wasteland full of land mines.

We learn that if we want to love and serve God and his people, we have to first learn to love and serve ourselves.

We learn that we needn't be afraid to love each other, to let our friendships nourish us.

We learn that being a nun doesn't require a denial that we are women first (p. 236).

When educated young sisters—who had been trained by Sister Formation and imbued with the spirit of the council— went out on mission, there was an explosion. Sisters who had studied Küng, Teilhard, Rahner, and each council document were sent to live and work among sisters whose training and experience were of the old order. Anyone who wants to know why those sisters left their congregations should read Wong's account of the kinds of experiences they had on mission.

Though she had been assigned to a "good house," she wrote, Wong soon found out that people were upset because she spent the "optional" recreation time in reading philosophy rather than talking to the old sisters. Sisters who had been educated before going out to teach were resented by those who did not have this opportunity. She and her friends went out of their way to drive sisters to appointments, volunteer for CCD, sit next to older sisters at recreation, etc. But this did not gain them the approval of the community. Their skirts were always too short, they had too much hair showing—the list goes on. When they worked for a poverty program and missed Mass or prayers or recreation, they were reprimanded and accused of dating men.

They were filled with zeal to reform the community, but finally realized that it would take longer than they could wait. Wong and other like-minded sisters, fired with the new ideas coming to them in council documents and other readings, met furtively to discuss their ideas and dream about reforming their congregations.

Each sister adapted to the new ideas that were in the air in the 1960s at her own speed. It was inevitable that change at different rates among different people would lead to clashes. Sociologists and anthropologists have much to tell us about the effects of rapid cultural change. What was unfortunate when this occurred in religious communities was that charity and other basic virtues of religious life sometimes were sadly lacking. This made the life unappealing to young women who were fired with zeal for living the gospel in an authentic way.

Many sisters who were educated according to the goals of the Sister Formation Movement have had experiences similar to those of Wong and her friends, experiences that finally caused them to leave religious life.

Conclusion

Dissatisfaction with community life and lack of personal fulfillment do indeed seem to have been important factors in many sisters' decisions to leave religious life. The existence of a healthy community life which provided ample scope for personal fulfillment and the authentic living of gospel values would undoubtedly have "saved" many of the vocations that were "lost."

Why was community life such a disappointment? Religious communities and the canon law which governed them failed to allow flexibility for adaptation to changing cultures and the assimilation of new knowledge. A static rather than a dynamic view of religious life prevailed. Prescriptions which focused on the letter of the law rather than its spirit, or imposed medieval western European customs on twentieth century American women, fostered a lifestyle which sometimes stifled the authentic living out of gospel values. At worst the result was an artificial "convent culture" which could only be maintained through brainwashing and milieu control—hardly an ambience for the development of mature Christian personalities or a healthy community life.

The Sister Formation Movement, by exposing sisters to contemporary thought in scripture, theology, anthropology, psychology, sociology, history and other fields, helped to bring about the demise of that restrictive convent culture which prevailed for so many decades of the twentieth century. Had not the Spirit moved the council fathers to call for a return to the founding charism and a renewal focused on the living of the gospel in the contemporary world, religious life would most likely have become increasingly more desiccated and lacking in significance for contemporary women and men.

So much for history. What of the present and the future? All who are concerned about American religious life must continue to struggle with questions like these: What constitutes a healthy community life? How can it be fostered? How best can sisters witness to gospel values in contemporary society?

The values of a particular time or culture must never again be imposed inappropriately on a different era or society, particularly since future epochs will be characterized by constant change and adaptation. Concepts such as ethnocentricity, acculturation, assimilation and culture clash must be part of the thinking of those who shape the church's pronouncements about religious life.

The signs of the times need to be studied not only by religious communities, but also by their bishops and members of the curia. Today there are many areas of service open to women who do not wish to take on the roles of wife and mother.

It is acceptable to be unmarried. In this age of lay ministry many have chosen to work for the church and serve humankind in such fields as Catholic schools, parishes, and social service, without embracing religious life or even celibacy.

A closer affiliation with the church and its hierarchy through entrance into religious life will not attract zealous young women if the church is seen to transgress basic human rights, to eschew due process, to violate freedom of conscience, to treat women like second-class citizens, and to summarily dismiss from their communities sisters whose work for the poor and study of the gospel imperative take them into the political arena.

There are many lessons to be learned from the trends studied here. Let us hope that they can enable religious communities to continue to serve the church and society and to foster an authentic spirituality among their members into future epochs.

Notes

1. Alexis de Toqueville, *Democracy in America,* ed. by Phillips Bradley (New York: Vintage, 1959), pp. 209ff.

2. Quoted in Clementine de la Corbiniere, *The Life and Letters of St. Francis Xavier* (Irma Le Fer de la Motte), trans. by the Sisters of Providence (Saint Mary-of-the-Woods, IN: Providence Press, 1934), p. 421.

3. Helen Rose Fuchs Ebaugh, *Out of the Cloister* (Austin: University of Texas Press, 1977), pp. 13ff.

4. Ibid., p. 3.

5. Ibid., pp. 5–6.

6. *Once There Was a Nun* (New York: Putnam, 1962), pp. 140ff.

7. Boston: Little, Brown, 1975.

8. Harper Colophon Books, 1984.

The Decline of Vocations in the United States

Reflections from a Psychological Perspective

Donna J. Markham, O.P.

The massive attrition of membership in religious congregations of men and women in the United States highlights several psychological research questions:

1. How are men and women religious perceived by the laity? Is this public image attractive to others?
2. What type of person is attracted to religious life today? Are there any significant psychological differences between male and female applicants?
3. Is it possible to predict, using psychological resources, which persons will remain in religious life and which persons will leave?

The comments that follow are based upon my research and will attempt to provide insights into the answers to these questions. Some comments are also offered on the conclusions drawn in the Neal and CARA studies. I would like to focus my attention on four areas.

First, a survey of lay persons' perceptions of religious and clergy will be examined, as this has particular bearing on the attraction and encouragement of vocations to religious life. The second section will focus on the psychological characteristics of applicants to religious congregations and will look at whether there are any significant psychological differences between male and female applicants who are currently applying. Third, a summary of a recent research project addressing the question of the predictability of perseverance in religious life will be examined. Finally, some reflections and possible directions will be explored.

I. Public Perceptions of Women Religious and Priests

It is a well established fact in group analytic theory that individuals seek to join groups to achieve common goals (i.e. engage in a group mission) and to satisfy certain needs for interaction and interdependency. A group may expect to attract new members who believe in its mission, observe a style of interaction which is consonant with their relational needs, and perceive a sense of interdependency (bonding, belonging) with the existing group membership constellation. That is, prospective members view the group as having good morale. A group will experience an attrition of its existing members and a lack of new membership when the corporate mission is unclear, the interactional style among the members is perceived as negative (e.g. superficial, critical, ambiguous), and cohesion and interdependency are insufficient to satisfy the needs of the members.

Given the radical decline in applicants to religious congregations, I undertook a study in 1981 to examine lay persons' collective perception of and attitudes toward religious to determine whether these groups were held in positive regard and were seen as attractive to potential members. The study did not include the laity's perception of religious men, but focused specifically on women religious and priests, and on women religious' and priests' perception of themselves. The study measured attitudes of 1,215 persons in sampling distributions according to age using the semantic differential technique, a subtle affective measure of attitude.

Randomization took into account *geographical region* (west, south, midwest, east), *setting* (urban, suburban, rural), and *ethnicity* (black, Hispanic, caucasian) of parishes and institutions which received questionnaires. In addition to the semantic differential instrument, a ten-item Likert summated rating scale was used to ascertain the sampling groups' cognitive attitudes toward specific areas of religious life or, in other words, what people *think* about religious life, as opposed to how they *feel* about religious life.

While a full explication of this study is beyond the scope of these comments, several conclusions are pertinent here:

1. Compared with other age groups (college women, single women 21–35 years, and others), high school girls viewed women religious least dynamically. The overall evaluation of the concept of religious women as dynamic and effective increased in a positive direction with age. Despite the high school sampling group's familiarity with sisters (the sample was drawn from parochial schools staffed by sisters), the group as a whole did not view sisters positively. This finding is in contradiction to Neal's suggestion that raising the entrance age has been a significant factor in explaining why there are now fewer applicants to the religious life. These data suggest that even if they could enter, high school girls are least attracted to religious life among the four groups surveyed.

2. All sampling groups, with the exception of women religious, evaluated priests significantly more positively than they evaluated women religious. This suggests a possible reason for the fact that priests and congregations of men religious are not experiencing as dire an attrition rate in vocations.

3. Women religious and priests view themselves more positively than others view them.

The results of this study indicate cause for serious concern about the endurance of women's congregations. These data suggest that if all factors remain constant, religious congregations will not gain adequate new membership and will continue to experience an attrition of current membership. These findings may offer some possible underlying reasons for the statistical findings cited in the Neal and CARA studies.

In examining research data related to the attitudes of women religious and lay persons toward women religious, there is apparent ambiguity among women religious themselves and among the laity concerning the *mission* of women religious. This ambiguity seems to exist in spite of the presence of well-documented and articulated mission statements. Further, there is an obvious and consistent discrepancy between attitudes which single lay women have toward women religious and which women religious have toward themselves. The most marked divergence concerns the assessment of the relative dynamism and vitality of religious life. Women religious think religious life is viable and dynamic; lay women do not.

The research data further indicate that there is a significant discrepancy between women religious' cognitive and affective evaluations of themselves. Women religious acknowledge concerns about the lack of clarity in living out the mission, discouragement with community life, concerns about not adequately serving the poor and disadvantaged, and moderate apprehension about the future of religious life. This cognitive response is suggestive of diminished morale and a kind of "corporate depression" which is highly defended against through the use of denial and reaction formation. This corporate defensive system was evidenced in women religious' responses to the subtle affective measure of attitude on the semantic differential. On this measure, they indicate feeling that they are a dynamic, active, powerful, and effective group. This affective evaluation is notably divergent from the three other groups of single women's assessment of women religious. These groups perceive women religious as rather good, not very dynamic, and not any more effective or progressive than priests or others. High school girls, college women, and single women aged 21–35 do not think or feel that women religious as a group are particularly attractive.

Research results indicate consistency between single women's cognitive and affective evaluations of women religious. Cognitive measures manifest considerable ambiguity concerning the mission of women religious and a marked degree of negativity toward becoming members.

Three conclusions concerning the continuance of religious life might be drawn from the results of this particular study:

1. There is need for clarification of the role and mission of women religious, both to members and to non-members, and a need to make a concerted effort on the part of members to exemplify that mission in their ministry and lifestyle.
2. An intensification of the positive value of belonging and bonding among members is needed if the institution of religious life is to attract a significantly greater number of members.
3. If religious are able to relinquish the intensity of their corporate defensive style of denial and reaction formation, it will occur only in an atmosphere of support from members and non-members. Situations which place religious in a position of feeling a need to validate and defend their lifestyle will only serve to provoke further the self-destructive end of maintaining

rigid defenses. That is, rather than assisting in the process of constructive change and evaluation, such criticism from external sources will likely intensify the rigidification of defenses, thereby resulting in heightened ineffectiveness and further demise.

II. Motivational Factors and Psychological Characteristics

After considering the laity's perception of men and women religious and the consequent attraction that congregations hold for potential members, an exploration of the applicants' primary conscious motivational factors leading to application was conducted. To gain additional insight into the emotional composition of applicants, further research was conducted using psychological test profiles of male and female applicants. In other words, an answer was sought to the question: What kind of person is attracted to religious life today, and for what reasons?

Examining data gleaned from depth clinical interviews of sixty-one females and forty-seven males who had applied to seventeen religious congregations in the midwest and Ontario during the past seven years, primary motivational factors were identified. Applicants were asked to respond to the question, "What is the one thing that prompts you to seek entrance into religious life today, rather than to pursue your life as a dedicated lay person in the church?" For purposes of clarity, the applicants' first responses to that question were noted and grouped under one of three headings:

A. Live a vowed life in community
    — live a simple lifestyle
    — pursue celibacy as a means toward closeness to God
    — give witness through community life
    — gain personal support through community

    — develop closer relationships with others in community

B.   Engage in the mission
    — minister to others
    — serve the poor, needy, under-served, oppressed
    — respond to the needs of the world
    — engage in corporate effort to respond to gospel imperative for justice and peace

C.   Develop a deeper prayer life
    — have opportunity for more contemplative life
    — deepen spirituality

While many applicants cited two or all three reasons for wanting to enter religious life, their primary reasons were tabulated, yielding the following results:

		M	F
A.	Vowed community life	56%	33%
B.	Mission	34%	59%
C.	Prayer life	10%	8%

These data indicate, then, that the primary conscious reason motivating women to seek entrance into religious congregations is to engage in the mission, while the primary reason men are seeking entrance is to pursue a vowed communal life. It might therefore be concluded that among those applying (not necessarily those accepted), there are definite needs and expectations, and that those needs and expectations differ according to sex. If those expectations are not met upon entrance, an attrition of membership can be expected. Women's congregations are more likely to attract and retain members if their mission is enfleshed in its members; men's congregations are more likely to attract and retain members if their community life is obvious and strong. While certainly there is a definite relationship between all three motivational factors, the question of emphasis and the concurrence between what is said and what is lived needs to be addressed.

While the conscious motivation of male and female applicants indicates differing emotional needs and expectations, further examination of applicants' psychological makeup lends additional insight into the question of who is seeking entrance into religious congregations today. Minnesota Multiphasic Personality Inventory (MMPI) profile scores of forty-four males and fifty-three females who have applied to fifteen religious congregations over the past seven years were analyzed and compared. Test data were gathered from the records of eight psychologists who are engaged in screening male and female applicants for religious life. Psychological testing was administered in all cases as a required component in admissions procedures for the various congregations. Mean ages for male and female applicants were 30.5 and 27.6 years, respectively. Data from applicants to diocesan seminaries were excluded from this study.

The MMPI is one of the most widely used objective psychological measures of emotional health in English-speaking countries. It is utilized routinely for screening applicants to a variety of vocations in which it is critical that emotional health be considered. As indicated, the MMPI is an objective instrument and therefore not subject to scoring differences due to diverse theoretical orientations of various psychological examiners. It is important to note that while individual scale scores are not as significant as the overall configuration of scores, the magnitude of elevation on the various scales is of significance. That is, the higher the score on the clinical scales, the greater the possibility of emotional distress.

Ninety-seven applicants' scores on the three validity scales and ten clinical scales were subjected to conservative, standard statistical analyses (*t*-tests, linear discriminant function analysis). No significant differences between males and females were found on the validity scales. These scales measure individuals' overall defensiveness, willingness to acknowledge emotional conflicts, and need to appear healthier or more disturbed than they actually are. Both men and women were equally open in responding to the test questions. Thus, differing response patterns of male and female applicants on the clinical scales was not due to higher levels of defensiveness by either group.

Analyses of scores on the clinical scales indicated statistically significant differences between males and females, with male applicants' scores always being in the more pathological direction. Highly significant differences were apparent on the Hs, Hy, Pa, Pt, and Sc scales (i.e. hypochondriasis, hysteria, paranoia, psychasthenia, and schizophrenia). Elevations over sixty-four on these scales are indicative of considerable emotional distress.

PERCENTAGE OF APPLICANTS SCORING OVER 65

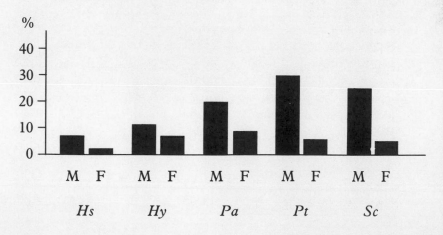

Actually, male and female applicants' scores differ so markedly that it is possible to predict with ninety-four percent accuracy the sex of the applicant based upon the configuration of scores (excluding the Mf, masculinity-femininity scale).

While these data reflect psychological profiles of applicants to religious congregations, it is not known which applicants were actually accepted by the various congregations. Further research is indicated to examine more clearly the psychological characteristics of persons who have been accepted. What is of concern is that among those attracted to religious life, there is considerable emotional distress. This is more apparent among male applicants. Of particular concern is the mean score of 72.57 on the Mf scale for males. This represents a mean in the third standard deviation among the norm and is suggestive of marked sex role confusion.

MMPI MEAN SCORES AND STANDARD DEVIATIONS

	MALES		FEMALES	
	Mean	*SD*	*Mean*	*SD*
Lie L Scale	49.75	8.03	49.60	9.11
Validity F	51.81	5.82	50.09	4.39
Correction K	60.81	9.21	60.15	6.52
Hypochondriasis	53.52	6.32	48.05	5.85
Depression	52.06	8.51	48.04	7.15
Hysteria	60.02	5.58	55.79	6.10
Psychopathic Deviate	61.23	9.20	56.83	7.53
Masculinity-femininity	72.57	9.58	47.77	9.21
Paranoia	59.84	5.12	56.15	5.69
Psychasthenia	60.22	9.70	51.75	6.90
Schizophrenia	59.68	10.94	52.83	5.52
Hypomania	60.20	8.16	55.90	7.88
Social introversion	44.07	9.00	43.87	6.88

Given the results of this study, it would seem imperative for admissions boards to evaluate carefully the psychological health of applicants so as to protect the individual from the unnecessary trauma caused by embarking upon a highly stressful lifestyle and also to protect congregations from the inclusion of more disturbed and problem-laden individuals.

III. Persistence Factors

While the previously-mentioned study examined the psychological characteristics of applicants, a recent study conducted by Watson (1985) explored whether, using psychological measures, it is possible to predict who is likely to persevere in religious life. The Watson study focused on an analysis of psychological profiles of women entering religious congregations after 1970. The Minnesota Multiphasic Personality Inventory (MMPI) was used, along with the Strong Campbell Interest Inventory and mental status examination data. While there is a limitation to the research (that is, the sample of thirty was small), from a methodological standpoint it is quite rigorous and statistically sound. For this reason, Watson's findings are of interest and value to this reflection on the decline of vocations.

When persisters were compared with non-persisters on the MMPI, no significant differences were noted on elevations of Validity, Correction, Depression, Hysteria, Hypochondriasis, Psychopathic Deviate, Psychasthenia, Schizophrenia, and Social Introversion scales. This finding contradicts the pre-Vatican II research of Barry (1960), Becker (1963), and Sherrin and Barrett (1963) who suggest that non-persisters indicate significantly higher scores on the clinical scales of the MMPI. That is, those researchers found that non-persisters were clinically not as healthy as persisters. On the basis of these studies, then, it may be concluded that women who are entering religious life today are psychologically different—that is, healthier—as a group than women who entered prior to renewal.

In particular, Watson found that post-Vatican II persisting women manifested significantly higher scores on the masculinity–femininity scale than non-persisting post-Vatican II women. Watson suggests that the persisting group might be described as rejecting the traditional feminine role, and as active and assertive in their relationships with others. They are also considered relaxed as a group and psychologically balanced (Graham, 1983).

The Watson study also cites a trend of elevated scores on the hypomanic scale for the persisting group, thereby suggesting that women who are energetic, talkative, creative, and rebelling against a stereotypical female role are better candidates to remain in religious life today. As individuals, post-Vatican II persisting women religious appear self-confident, gregarious, and psychologically healthy.

The final trend cited in Watson's research is a lower L (lie) validity score among persisters. Watson suggests that the persisting group responded frankly to questions, were confident in admitting shortcomings, and were independent and socially responsive. There were no significant differences between the persisters and non-persisters on the Ego Strength, Religious Vocation, or Dominance scales of the MMPI. Analyses of demographic and background data did not reveal any significant differences between the two groups, nor did mental status examination results.

Watson's findings support the research of Weisgerber (1969) which suggested the need for additional investigation of the Mf and Ma configuration with religious. It is interesting to note that Weisgerber's research, based on data collected prior to Vatican II (1950–1963), describes the same trends that Watson found but located them among the *non-persisting* group of religious. Before the renewal of religious life, more assertive, creative, and outspoken persons were more likely to leave, according to Weisgerber's findings.

It is important to note that, among women accepted for entrance into religious congregations, both persisters and nonpersisters represent a psychologically healthy group. Given such a psychologically healthy group of women religious, it is extremely difficult, if not impossible, to predict from psychological factors alone who will persist. A replication of the Watson study, using a larger sample, would be extremely helpful in the further exploration of this question.

IV. Reflections

In considering the material included in the Neal and CARA studies, as well as the data cited in the research projects just discussed, several conclusions can be drawn. First, I believe that the continuation of celibate religious community life (as we know it) beyond the present generation is questionable. Younger persons do not find religious life attractive. Among the small group of persons who apply, there is evidence of considerable emotional distress, especially among male applicants. Members of religious congregations are themselves unclear about their mission in the church and in the world. The lack of internal clarity and the presence of marked negative regard and criticism from external sources result in stressed organizational functioning characterized by depression, denial, and unconscious attempts to cover over critical concerns.

Second, contrary to the CARA conclusions that large congregations of men are likely to attract a greater number of vocations when they have a mission statement, a diversity of ministries, a more liberal stance, and a full-time vocation director, the experience of women's congregations seems to be different. Women's congregations meeting these criteria do not seem to be gaining significantly greater numbers than congregations which do not meet the CARA criteria. Very few women are entering either, but these women are psychologically healthy. The research data suggest that, with regard to women's congregations, motivation for and attraction to religious life is closely related to the congregation's apparent living-out of the mission.

It is in a radical response to the mission of Jesus that celibate religious life in community seems to hold attraction for women today. By radical response, the criteria for ministry becomes a deliberate commitment to respond to human need in those areas where others cannot or will not venture—areas of particular need which have been left unattended. For example, such an immersion in the mission could, by necessity, urge religious to enter into ministry in geographical settings that are impoverished and/or dangerous, urge religious to take political positions in radical support of human rights, even when such positions are unpopular, highly conflictual, and counter-cultural, and impel religious to venture into those areas where financial resources, physical comfort, and safety are precarious, if not altogether lacking. Using such criteria for ministry, religious would first determine whether others would be able and willing to enter into that "place." If that were the case, then the vowed religious would choose to go elsewhere.

Celibacy takes on an emergent meaning insofar as the single person does not place a spouse or children in this atmosphere. The celibate commits only his or her own life to this mission. Further, it would seem impossible to engage in this radical response to critical human need without the support of a faith community. Within this context, celibate religious community may have particular meaning and value.

It may also be important for congregations to explore alternative modes of membership which do not require vowed commitment of poverty, chastity and obedience to God through the institutional church. Given the emphasis which female applicants place on participation in the mission, it may be that promises of solidarity in mission, made to the religious congregation, may provide a framework for non-vowed commitment to religious congregations.

Regardless of what choices are made concerning future commitment to the gospel as members of religious congregations, the personal and corporate conversion of heart that is needed if such a concerted radical response can be made will not occur without painstaking self-evaluation and fidelity to the consequences of such reflection and evaluation. Obviously, such a conversion experience cannot be mandated, nor can it be expected that all persons in religious life today would be desirous or capable of such a radical response. Compassionate understanding, non-judgmental respect, and support of all members whose varying ways of giving expression to their religious commitment co-exist within the institution of religious life today are crucial. Such witness to collaboration, charity, loyalty, and bonding is a hallmark of a truly Christian community. It is in this atmosphere that fear and anxiety are diminished, thus preparing the way for the more disturbing aspects of depth change to surface and be addressed.

References

Barry, W. (1960). *An MMPI Scale for Seminary Candidates.* Unpublished master's thesis, Fordham University, New York.

Becker, A. (1963). "A study of the personality traits of successful religious women of teaching orders." In *The Twentieth*

Yearbook of the National Council of Measurement in Education, 20, 124–125.

Cartwright, D. and Zander, A. (1966). *Group Dynamics, Research and Theory*. New York: Harper and Row.

Graham, J. (1983). *The MMPI: A Practical Guide*. New York: Oxford University Press.

Markham, D. (1983). "Linear Progressive Model of Group Treatment of the Borderline Patient." In *Proceedings: Adult Psychiatric Day Treatment Symposium*. Minneapolis: University of Minnesota Press.

Markham, D. (1981). *An Analysis of Members' and Non-Members' Attitudes Toward Women Religious*. Unpublished paper.

Osgood, C., Suci, G., and Tannenbaum, P. (1973). *The Measurement of Meaning*. Urbana: University of Illinois Press.

Shaw, M. (1975). *Group Dynamics*. New York: McGraw-Hill.

Watson, P. (1985). *Persistence Factors in Vocational Choice*. Unpublished doctoral dissertation, University of Detroit.

Weisgerber, C. (1969). *Psychological Assessment of Candidates for a Religious Order*. Chicago: Loyola University Press.

Religious Life in the United States

Reflections of a Cultural Anthropologist

Gerald A. Arbuckle, S.M.

Cultural anthropology is the only social science discipline which claims to deal with culture systematically. Hence, it is from the angle of culture and culture change that I will approach the questions of what has happened to religious life since Vatican II and why vocation recruitment is so low.

I will first define what is meant by culture and suggest a relevant model of culture change. I will then attempt to formulate an anthropological model to describe what happened to religious life after the mid-1960s. I do not *prove* anything. Rather, I remain on the level of "anthropological hunches" supported at times with faith reflections. I leave it to the readers to decide whether or not my hunches fit their own experience.[1]

In summary form, my thesis is: Anthropologically, much of the turmoil within religious congregations since the council was to have been expected, in consequence of dramatic value and cultural changes. Secondly, I hold to Mircea Eliade's view that cultures generally experience cyclic regressions to chaos as a preface to a new creativity.[2] I believe that the type of chaos described by Eliade exists in religious life today; I also claim that out of this chaos there willl emerge a more radical expression of the gospel message. The quality of religious life will rise, but not vocation recruitment numbers.

Anthropological Reflections on Culture and Culture Change

Culture is something living, something giving vital meaning, direction, identity, to people in ways that touch not just the mind, but especially the heart. The anthropologist tries to uncover pivotal symbols—that is, symbols that form the very foundation of the culture. If they are destroyed or gravely undermined, especially within a short period of time, then the consequences for the people and their institutions can be traumatic. People lose their sense of identity, belonging and direction. Disorientation symptoms show themselves at the individual and at the group levels, e.g. anger, anomie, frustration, violence, enthusiasm for quick and "miraculous" solutions to identity crises and the loss of a sense of belonging.

An Interpretative Model of the Post-Vatican II Church in the United States

A "model," or frame of reference, in cultural anthropology is very much a construct by a researcher used to facilitate a better understanding of very complex situations. A model reflects reality to the extent that it highlights certain emphases or trends. A model does not attempt to include details which would or could obscure the emphases.

Prior to Vatican II the American church was "the best organized and most powerful of the nation's subcultures—a source of both alienation and enrichment for those born within it and an object of bafflement or uneasiness for others."[3] The sub-culture disintegrated in its original form from the mid-1960s onward because of the combined interaction of two major revolutions (though signs of some disintegration were evident prior to this time, e.g. the upward mobility of Catholics educationally, economically and socially). The dramatic nature of the breakdown resulted from the interaction of forces coming from:

☐ the cultural revolution of expressive disorder in the wider American society;

☐ the theological and cultural revolution from within the church itself.

Only now are we beginning to appreciate more objectively the extraordinary nature and long-term effects of the revolution of expressive disorder. A country that had prided itself, for example, on its political stability found its political system no longer equal to meeting the demands for change. New forms of protest and communication emerged, unheard of before, e.g. massive protest meetings.[4] In the arts, education, literature, religion, the boundaries that suffered the most vigorous and successful attacks were those between public and private spheres, between decent and indecent, tabooed and available, sacred and profane, between good taste and vulgarity, male and female. The ideological rejection of control typically showed itself in a preference for randomness over plan or structure, for excess over balance, for subjective over the objective mode, for emotion over reason, for the immediate satisfaction over sacrifice.[5]

Some powerful symbols of American culture became yet more dominant, e.g. individualism, the cult of self-fulfillment, consumerism.[6] And from this period also "youth culture" became a sociological and commercial reality.[7]

The theological emphases of Vatican II and later need not be spelled out here. It is sufficient to note that from a theological stance, where God and the world were viewed as opposites and specifically Christian values were stressed more especially than human values, Vatican II moved the church back to a position of dialogue with the world and to the search for justice and peace.[8] If the times had been less revolutionary the church might have been able to have adjusted itself to the world with a little less turmoil than in fact it experienced. The church opened itself to a world in change, but in addition to a world in *traumatic* change.

The Need for Refounding Persons

After Vatican II there was a brief period of euphoria among Catholics, including priests and religious. Theoretically, the theological emphases seemed acceptable and well received. Adjustments to religious life culture were made. But the optimism was misplaced. It would take very deep personal and corporate conversion and changes for the restructuring of rules to be effective. Following the brief and attempted adjustment, the sense of frustration began to emerge, sometimes forcefully. The changes that had taken place did not produce the new-style religious communities and apostolates that seemed so easily possible earlier. Ecclesiastical authorities—the pope, bishops, religious superiors—became objects of public attack particularly from within the church itself.[9] This was an entirely new phenomenon in modern times. Pivotal symbols of authority within the traditional immigrant church took a severe beating. If the church was to grow within the American culture, then new symbols, or old symbols with modified meanings, would have to develop. Fundamental to these symbols would be the theological emphasis on the mission of the church to the world.

Given this background, what would an anthropological observer have expected to have happened to religious life in America? Within the traditional Catholic subculture, religious houses, provinces and congregations were par excellence examples of organized cultural identity; religious clearly knew why they existed—boundaries between them and the laity and between them and the world were very clearly and symbolically marked. These religious-life cultures felt the full impact of the revolutionary changes within and outside the church. Symptoms of culture shock on the part of many religious would have been logically expected. Culture shock describes the cognitive and psychological crisis which can arise with the encounter of one culture with dramatically powerful forces of change; new ways of ordering reality and rendering it intelligible are suddenly imposed on a people or otherwise disrupt its accustomed patterns of thinking and identity. I suspect that culture shock would have influenced the decisions of many religious to withdraw in at least five ways:

1. The General Loss of Meaning.

If people over-identify with structures and their symbols, then when these structures are destroyed or seriously undermined the same people are apt to lose meaning and purpose in their lives. Religious were confronted with the theological reality that *all* people—clerics, religious, laity—are called to holiness. With structures no longer supporting their way of feeling more perfect and different from lay people, and with the revitalized notion of being radical for the Lord (often overlooked), many religious fell into a state of malaise. If they could not find their way out of this confusion, they sought another way of life, very frequently the lay world, which they thought would give them meaning.

2. Cultural Romanticism.

Cultural romanticism is the uncritical acceptance of cultural symbols either in one's culture or in another culture. The cultural symbols of self-fulfillment and individualism—given such vigorous encouragement in the expressive revolution—would have appeared far more attractive and humanly ideal to many religious as they looked in their enthusiasm at the world to be evangelized. People who are caught up in a cultural disintegration experience find objective and critical reflection difficult, if not impossible at times.

3. The Removal of Social Sanctions.

In a culture where the boundaries dividing people from other cultures or subcultures are rigidly defined, there are clearly established legal and/or social pressures against withdrawal. Once the culture begins to disintegrate these sanctions weaken. So also with the American Catholic subculture. It became socially easier for people to leave religious life when they no longer felt the social stigma of former times if they left.[10]

4. Dissatisfaction with the Pace of Renewal.

For several years following Vatican II there were general and provincial chapters of renewal. Fine documents were written. Great hope was expressed in these written statements and in new legislation incorporating the key theological emphases, e.g. the social justice apostolate, the renewal of the spiritual life. These documents, together with the follow-up seminars and workshops, became endowed with almost magical or millennial expectations. John Futreall, I feel, is making this point when he writes of the late 1960s: "It was felt that adaptation through changing external structures would result in deep interior renewal. Indeed, for many the degree of renewal was measured by the number of external changes."[11] Intense frustration developed for some religious once they realized that the external changes were not effecting the magical results expected of them. Without understanding the slow pace of real change and lacking the spirituality suitable for the situation, it is little wonder if people eventually felt that they had no vocation within religious life.

5. *Poverty of Initial Formation.*

Religious were trained in the period leading up to Vatican II to assume that the church culture (and therefore religious culture) never changed. Hence, it was only rarely that religious were taught subjects, like the social sciences, that specifically aimed to help people understand and cope with change. On the contrary, such subjects were considered dangerous and philosophically subversive. Answers to pastoral problems were pre-packaged in manuals on morals which rarely changed their contents from decade to decade. Nor was the spiritual training of candidates attuned to preparing them for social and cultural change. I would strongly support the view, therefore, that "if some 40,000 priests and religious have 'given up' in the last ten years it is not least of all because they had not been prepared for the cultural, sociological, and theological changes that called everything into question. This is why they could not cope with the changes."[12]

Difficulties in Vocation Recruitment.

In a cultural malaise or culture shock situation, people are open to whatever can give them identity, a sense of belonging, and direction in life. People respond to individuals and movements that confidently spell out a purpose in life. The articulation is both verbal and in action. If people who claim to lead are in any way unsure of their goals in life, then this uncertainty will be detected and their leadership rejected.[13]

Some claim that Catholic youth have become so immersed in the symbols of individualism, materialism and the cult of self-fulfillment that religious life simply is no longer attractive. Dean Hoge and others, however, note that at the same time as Catholic vocations fall off Protestant seminaries are full. "This situation suggests," they claim, "that particular aspects of the Catholic Church or subculture, not the recent values of the youth culture, are most decisive in influencing vocation trends."[14] I believe that there are four major aspects at least in the present Catholic subculture that are obstructing vocation recruitment:

- ☐ The meaning and goals of religious life are not clear enough to many religious; their uncertainty does not attract vocations.
- ☐ More refounding persons have yet to emerge within existing congregations.
- ☐ There are still an insufficient number of concrete pastoral programs that relate the gospel to the most urgent needs within the American culture.
- ☐ Vocation recruitment advertising reflects uncertainty as to goals of religious life.

Because of the limitations of space, I will expand here only on the aspect of the need for more refounding persons to emerge.

Historically, refounding people are those who have the gift to see the enormity of the gap between the gospel and reality. They are also practical, creatively imaginative, prophetic people, because in a spirit of enormous love of the Lord they are able to work out how this gap can be bridged.

Change takes place because individuals are able to motivate others along certain lines. This is true in religious life also. Whole communities do not initiate changes; individuals instead act as the dynamic catalysts and draw others to join them in the change process. The type of person we need as change agents in religious congregations have precisely the qualities we detect in our own founders and foundresses: a deep love of the Lord expressed in prayer and action, a firm grasp and love of the charism of the congregation, pastoral versatility and creativity, a certain faith stubbornness, experience of deep suffering in the Lord, accompanied at times by their being rejected or marginalized by members of their own congregation. They are patient people as they know that change in depth and quality occurs slowly. Radical conversion is rarely a sudden or dramatic event.[15] I deliberately use the words "*re*founders" and "*re*foundresses" in order to highlight the dramatic qualities of the people I see as essential if religious congregations are to survive and grow in the service of the church. The present chaotic uncertainty in religious congregations today demands the type of person I describe.[16]

Hence, the task of refounding persons is first to call us to reconversion to the Lord. Second, they invite us to join with them in pastoral initiatives that relate the gospel message to a world markedly different from that known to the founding persons. I think we are still very uncomfortable with the thought of living with such people. We still feel that in some way or other more chapters, committee meetings, or apostolic task forces will lead the congregation to new life. The anthropology of change does not support this assumption.

Congregational leaders in particular have the duty to discern the presence of refounding people (if they exist at all, they will be few in number) and then place them within the congregation in positions in which they can have the most positive influence. Generally, they should not be over-burdened with administrative duties, but given space and time for creative action. Put them well away from existing houses of the congregation so that they do not have to waste energy constantly legitimizing what they are doing to others of the congregation.

Until such people emerge in sufficient numbers, I expect recruitment to congregations of creatively committed candidates to remain low or non-existent. Paul VI writes that "modern man listens more willingly to witnesses than to teachers, and if he does listen to teachers, it is because they are witnesses."[17] Dean Hoge's overview of research suggests that priests and religious are not giving the encouragement in vocation recruit-

ment that is desirable.[18] We religious desperately need refounding people to witness to what religious life today *should*
be. Our hesitancy to encourage people to join us will not
disappear until people of the caliber I am speaking of emerge
(and are allowed to emerge) within our midst.

I have concentrated on refounding persons. Yet, similar
points could be made about the emergence of new congregations. Generally speaking, it may be easier to establish new
congregations than to revitalize existing ones. Congregational
cultures are often vigorously opposed to change of the reform-
ist quality needed.[19]

Conclusion

I am basically confident about the future of religious life
in the United States. This does not mean that I believe that
this or that congregation will necessarily survive and grow. In
fact, my hunch is that many provinces, even congregations,
will die, not because God necessarily wishes them to die or that
their mission is finished, but because they do not have the
heart to confront in faith the darkness within as the preface for
creativity in the Lord. Radical gospel living will be characteristic of religious communities in the future; for this reason, if for
no other, I do not think religious congregations will attract
large numbers again.

I believe that from the present confusion following such
dramatic cultural changes there will emerge individuals within
accepting congregations (or they will establish new communities) who have the faith, courage and gospel vision of our
founding persons. These people will call us to conversion of a
radical gospel nature, marked by a strong counter-cultural
quality. They will invite us to join with them in revitalizing
apostolic communities that will be noted for their pastoral
flexibility, mobility and creativity. These individuals will be

the powerless ones of the Lord, those whom we least expect to be blessed with the gifts that summon the rest of us to conversion and mission in the world. There is little hope for religious congregations without such people.

Humanly speaking, the insight of cultural anthropology is that it was necessary for us to wait this length of time since Vatican II to come to an awareness of precisely how real revitalization and refounding takes place. God of course could have entered the process of cultural adjustment more directly and dramatically. Normally, however, he lets the process of chaos, confusion and cultural adjustment take its "natural" course. He "adapts" to the human condition; he invites us to read freely the signs of the times. We either freely accept or reject this invitation.

> You must go by the way of dispossession.
> In order to arrive at what you are not . . .
> *T.S. Eliot*[20]

Notes

1. The major themes of this essay are considered more at length by the author in "Why They Leave: Reflections of a Religious Anthropologist," in *Review for Religious*, Vol. 42, No. 6, 1983, pp. 815–830, and in *Strategies for Growth in Religious Life*, New York: Alba House, 1987.

2. See Mircea Eliade, *Myth and Reality*, New York: Harper & Row, 1975, pp. 39–53, 184–193, and *The Myth of the Eternal Return*, London: Routledge and Kegan Paul, 1955, Chapters 2 and 3.

3. John Cogley, *Catholic America*, New York: Image, 1974, p. 135.

4. See the following helpful studies: Milton Viorst, *Fire in the Streets: America in the 1960s*, New York: Simon and

Schuster, 1979; Morris Dickstein, *Gates of Eden: American Culture in the Sixties*, New York: Basic Books, 1975; Peter Clecak, *America's Quest for the Ideal Self: Dissent and Fulfillment in the 60s and 70s*, New York: Oxford University Press, 1983.

5. See Bernice Martin, *A Sociology of Contemporary Cultural Change*, Oxford: Basil Blackwell, 1981, p. 112 and passim.

6. See Robert N. Bellah et al., *Habits of the Heart: Individualism and Commitment in American Life*, New York: Harper & Row, 1986, pp. 142–163 and passim.

7. See Michael Blake, *Comparative Youth Culture: Sociology of Youth Culture and Youth Subcultures in America, Britain and Canada*, London: Routledge and Kegan Paul, 1985, pp. 83–104.

8. See G.A. Arbuckle, "Inculturation Not Adaptation: Time To Change Terminology," in *Worship*, Vol. 60, No. 6, 1986, pp. 511–520.

9. See George A. Kelly, *The Battle for the American Church*, New York: Doubleday, 1981, pp. 9–20.

10. In the terminology of anthropologist Mary Douglas, church culture moved from a state of "strong group/strong grid" to "weak group/weak grid." See Mary Douglas, *Natural Symbols: Explorations in Cosmology*, New York: Random House, 1970, pp. 98–106.

11. "The Future of Religious Life: Challenge to Leadership and Formation," in *Human Development*, 1982, Vol. 2, p. 5.

12. Cited by Walbert Buhlmann, *The Chosen Peoples*, Middlegreen: St. Paul Publications, 1982, p. 273.

13. See Thomas J. Peters and Robert H. Waterman, *In Search of Excellence: Lessons from America's Best-Run Companies*, New York: Harper & Row, 1982, pp. 272–291.

14. *Research on Men's Vocations to the Priesthood and the*

Religious Life, Washington: U.S. Catholic Conference, 1984, p. 331.

15. See Evelyn M. Woodward, "On the Grim Periphery: Reflections on Marginality and Alienation," in *Review for Religious*, Vol. 45, No. 5, 1983, pp. 709–711.

16. See G.A. Arbuckle, *Strategies for Growth in Religious Life*, ibid., pp. 23–66.

17. Ibid., par. 41.

18. Ibid., p. 54.

19. See G.A. Arbuckle, "Innovation in Religious Life," in *Human Development*, Vol. 6, No. 3, 1985, pp. 45–49.

20. "East Coker," in *Four Quartets*, London: Faber and Faber, 1959, p. 25.

A Canonical Perspective on the Departures from Religious Life

Rose McDermott, S.S.J.

Undoubtedly there are many factors in the socio-cultural and ecclesial constructs which effect departures from and the scarcity of vocations to religious life. These issues have been dealt with by experts in theology, history, ecclesiology, sociology, and the behavioral sciences.[1] However, there are significant issues within the framework of religious life itself which seemingly have influenced the decisions of members to depart from or of potential candidates to decline entering a particular religious institute. Many of these internal issues fare prominently in the Neal/CARA studies.[2]

The church called religious institutes to renewal and adaptation during the Second Vatican Council. During these approximately twenty years the members through the appropriate internal structures have examined and adjusted the constitutive elements of their lifestyle according to gospel spirituality, conciliar teaching, their own particular charism, contemporary society, and the needs of the people of God. At times and in particular instances, the particular identity of a religious institute has been blurred in this process. The ambiguity clouding the identity of a religious institute has had traumatic implications for some members of these institutes for it has brought into sharp focus the fundamental question of their vocation to the institute. Likewise, the blurring of the identity of the religious institute has had serious ramifications on the decisions of potential candidates seeking to unite their personal call from

God with what they perceive to be the gift or communal vocation of a particular religious institute for the life and mission of the church. It is no easy thing to give oneself to a permanent commitment in these rapidly changing times. But observable ambiguity and instability in the lifestyle one is considering makes the decision more difficult, if not impossible.

It should be noted here from a canonical viewpoint that the struggle during this time of transition is particularly acute in apostolic institutes of women religious. The norms of the 1917 Code of Canon Law did not adequately provide for significant aspects of these congregations of women religious whose apostolic activity is rooted in the very nature of the institute.[3] Many of these women religious are only today discovering the true gift and potential of their particular institute for the church. Hence, the renewal and adaptation called for by the church is of a more radical and complex nature for women religious than for their male counterparts.

This essay will point to constitutive elements of religious life which have been studied, renewed, and adapted according to the lived experience of the religious and the principles of conciliar and post-conciliar documents. At times, tension and uncertainty in the reformulation and adaptation of these elements in the constitutions and lived experience of the religious have effected severe vocational problems, both within and beyond the particular religious lifestyle. I have approached the question of departures from and the scarcity of vocations to religious life only from a canonical perspective and from my experience with religious in an Office of Vicar for Religious for seven years (1979–1986).

I. *Ecclesial and Institutional Membership*

Conciliar and post-conciliar teachings have contextualized religious institutes in the life and mission of the church:

> Rather it (religious life) should be seen as a form of
> life to which some Christians, both clerical and lay,
> are called by God so that they may enjoy a special gift
> of grace in the life of the Church and may contribute,
> each in his own way, to the saving mission of the
> Church.[4]

This emphasis on the ecclesial identity and responsibility of religious institutes and their members to the church is in keeping with the conciliar understanding of the church as the community of the people of God. The role of religious in the life and mission of the church is expressed in the norms of the 1983 Code of Canon Law,[5] and is a marked change from the former law wherein neither the ecclesial role of religious nor their apostolate was explicitly stated.[6]

In addition to centering religious life in the heart of the church, conciliar teachings have stressed the importance of the particular gift or charism of a religious institute:

> Each authentic charism brings an element of real
> originality in the spiritual life of the Church along
> with the fresh initiatives for action.[7]

The safeguard and fostering of the particular gift of a religious institute and the employment of the principle of subsidiarity were major considerations in the revision of the church law for consecrated life.[8] Repeatedly, the *ius proprium* or proper law of the religious institute is referred to the revised code.[9] It is interesting to note that the proposed 1977 schema on consecrated life was rejected because of its seeming blurring of the particular charisms of religious institutes through a too general description of particular charisms of consecrated life in the church.[10]

At times, the renewal of charism and the revision of the

proper law of a religious institute were conducted without sufficient consideration or apart from the institute's identity as an ecclesial community. This omission can encourage a certain narcissism, since the renewal efforts of the religious were not recognized as important for the whole people of God. The failure in the past to contextualize a religious institute as an ecclesial reality, and the confusion at present over conciliar ecclesiology, greatly augment this problem. The lack of ecclesial awareness was particularly noticeable in many apostolic institutes of women religious.

In the past, these women religious lived a semi-cloistered existence moving from convent to school or hospital. Limited opportunities for education in theology and participation in the mission of the church provided little understanding of ecclesial membership and responsibility. Since the Second Vatican Council, these religious have generally accepted the concept of church as a community. However, many factors and experiences, both in the past and in the present, preclude their accepting unreservedly the structures and processes of the church. Their approach to the church and their reservations frequently place these women religious in adversarial positions vis-à-vis those whose training and comprehension of the church is of a more hierarchical framework. Women religious see themselves as second class citizens or servants in the church; their ideas, concerns, and suggestions are not taken seriously by church authorities, and they are excluded from the decision-making bodies in the church. These reasons prevent an emphasis on ecclesiology in the renewal and adaptation of some religious institutes of women religious. This is undeniably regrettable, since religious life depends on the church for its life, nurturance, and mission.

Sometimes tensions arise when religious institutes emphasize ecclesial membership without taking due cognizance of their particular charism in the renewal process. This approach

213

may arise from (a) disillusionment with the internal renewal process, (b) lack of in-depth study into the charism and patrimony of the institute resulting in ambiguity around its proper identity, or (c) failure to see the potential of the institute's charism in the context of present-day reality in the church and society. The over-emphasis on ecclesial membership to the detriment of the particular gift of the institute within the context of the church seems reactionary to the past when religious, particularly women, played little if any role in the broader arena of the church. In any event, this uneven approach to renewal proves unproductive for the institute and its members as well as for the church. Since the identity of the particular institute is nebulous, the church loses the witness of the particular gift of an institute which should be a significant contribution to its life and holiness. In such renewal efforts, the blurring of the distinction between the role of the laity and these religious posits a further concern.

II. Consecration and Mission

There exists a dynamic unity between consecration and mission in religious life. Conciliar and post-conciliar documents reflect this relationship between the two realities:

> They (religious) have dedicated their whole lives to his service. This constitutes a special consecration, which is deeply rooted in their baptismal consecration and is a fuller expression of it. Since this gift of themselves has been accepted by the Church, they should be aware that they are dedicated to its service also.[11]

Some authors on religious life tend to deal with consecration to the neglect of mission, or stress mission to the exclusion of consecration. They fail to point out that the responsibility and fruit of consecration is mission, and/or that the mission of a religious is rooted in the consecration and distinctive spirituality of his or her institute. Sometimes, too, religious tend to forget the dynamic unity of these constitutive elements of their lives.

Since the Second Vatican Council, one can find a renewed interest among some religious regarding aspects of their life pertaining to a special consecration: intense personal prayer, prolonged directed retreats, frequent spiritual direction, shared faith experience, extended sojourns in houses of prayer, and meaningful liturgy. Exemplary as these spiritual activities are, they cannot be separated from the responsibility of religious to the life and mission of the church. Such a concentration in the renewal process cannot become an escape from the inevitable tension and transition effected by changes in the adaptation of the religious lifestyle to present-day realities. The approach of religious to spirituality should be congruent with the nature and end of their particular institutes. To accept a spirituality which implies a radical shift away from the charism of the institute would only invite confusion in the other members and those outside the institute, and mar the identity of the specific religious institute. Elitism, alienation, and disorientation among the members could result.

Conciliar teaching, particularly *Gaudium et spes*, the Pastoral Constitution on the Church in the Modern World, has sensitized religious to the cry of the poor and the demands of social justice. This awareness has prompted much activity on the part of religious, even to extremes at times, in order to alleviate the poverty surrounding them in the developed and the developing countries. If the activity of religious is not rooted in the spirituality of their particular charism, if it is divorced from the nature of the institute to which the religious belongs, or if it is not supported by the administration and other members of the religious institute, the labor can eventually lead to fragmentation in the life of the member and severance from his or her institute. The church has experienced the phenomenon today of religious refusing to be missioned to certain apostolic activities with subsequent departures from their institutes to participate in political or social causes beyond the limits of the apostolic dimension of the religious institute. Apostolic activities of both religious institutes and their members should be reassessed in light of their proper charism and the church in today's world. It is the task of religious institutes to clarify their distinctive identity in the church vis-à-vis the lay people who, having received the sacraments of Christian initiation, accept their responsibilities in the life and mission of the church.

A theology of religious life which takes full cognizance of the delicate balance of consecration and mission would avoid the blurring of the identity of a religious institute and prevent vocational difficulty on the part of a member.

Certainly all religious, like the rest of the baptized, are called to holiness and intimate union with God. But if a significant number of the members fail in this continual conversion to Christ according to the particular spirituality of the institute, the very charism of the institute can be stifled. There is no charism of a religious institute unless it is articulated in the lives and apostolic activity of the members.

Religious, like the rest of the baptized, share in the teaching, sanctifying and governing mission of the church. However, their participation in this mission is conditioned by the nature and end of their respective religious institutes. For an institute to fail to respond to the cry of the poor or the needs of God's people according to its own nature and gifts, or for individual religious to engage in apostolic activity without appropriate consultation and missioning by the legitimate authority of the religious institute, would seriously jeopardize the identity of the institute and its apostolic activity in the mission of the church.

III. Traditional and New Ministries

The church's teaching has been consistent in exhorting religious to be faithful to their traditional apostolates, while remaining open to the possibility of new ministries as articulated by the present-day needs of the people of God. The 1983 Code of Canon Law reflects this teaching in one of its norms on the apostolate of religious:

> Superiors and members are faithfully to retain the mission and works proper to the institute; nevertheless they are to accommodate these prudently to the needs of times and places, including the use of new and appropriate means.[12]

Sociocultural changes, technological advances, developments in behavioral sciences, a heightened sensitivity to social justice, and the professional potential of older candidates for religious life have affected the ministry of religious institutes in the church.

Traditional ministries, such as social services, health care, and formal education, have been carried out by religious through the centuries. The sophistication of today's society precludes an outdated or naive undertaking of these perennial services; rather, it demands a continued reexamination of these apostolates of religious in accordance with the signs of the times, professional development, the nature of the religious institute, and the present potential of the members. For religious to fail in such an important and demanding undertak-

217

ing would be a disservice to the people of God and a disregard for the apostolic spirit rooted in the very nature of their institutes.

At times, religious institutes abandon traditional ministries without a detailed study of the people's needs and their members' potential to continue the service. At times there is no valid reason for withdrawing from a traditional service, e.g. no personnel to fill the positions. Such actions leave the people of God in need and disbelief. In some cases, members of religious institutes opt for ministries other than the traditional one(s) served by the institute. If these apostolates are a radical departure from the nature and end of the institute, if the individual religious fails to understand his or her relationship to the legitimate superior in the missioning process, or to his or her community in a life of mutual support—or if the needs of the church are not a priority—this change in apostolic activity can seriously weaken the institute. Subsequent changes in lifestyle, such as living alone in an apartment or living with another religious institute, the lack of common and/or community life, and incompetence in a new ministry, discourage individual members and can lead to a loss of vocation and the blurring of the identity of the institute.

The expansion of ministries in the church since the Second Vatican Council, the scarcity of clerics, the educational background and potential of religious, the recognized role of laity in the mission of the church, and the new needs of God's people have led religious into specialized ministries beyond the traditional ones mentioned above. Women religious, particularly, have entered ministries in the sanctifying, teaching, and governing roles of the church heretofore served by priests only. The presence of women religious in these areas of service has presented the church more clearly as community and opened channels of dialogue and collaboration for these women religious with bishops and other clerics.

Here it must be noted that the most diligent efforts on the part of religious institutes for the renewal and adaptation of apostolic services in a diocese will remain ineffectual if there is a lack of pastoral planning on the diocesan level. The diocesan bishop should afford the best possible consultation for major superiors of religious institutes as they deal with the concerns of their traditional apostolates and the challenge of new ministries in the diocese. Pastoral planning at the diocesan level can provide for mutual relations and collaboration among the clergy, religious and laity of the local church, while removing competition, mistrust and secrecy from what should be everyone's concern for the good of the church. Likewise, such planning can encourage shared resources, avoid the duplication of efforts, and effect harmonious, efficient service to the entire community of God's people in a particular church.

IV. Common and Community Life

The 1983 Code of Canon Law reflects the importance of community life for institutes of consecrated life:

> The life of brothers or sisters proper to each institute, by which all members are united together like a special family in Christ, is to be determined in such a way that it becomes a mutual support for all in fulfilling the vocation of each member. Moreover by their communion as brothers or sisters, rooted in and built on love, the members are to be an example of universal reconciliation in Christ.[13]

Likewise, the code reflects the importance of life in common for religious institutes:

A religious institute is a society in which members, according to proper law, pronounce public vows either perpetual or temporary, which are to be renewed when they have lapsed, and live a life in common as brothers or sisters.[14]

By community life could be understood all of the realities which religious share as (a) human beings created in the image of God, (b) Christians baptized into the body of Christ, and (c) religious incorporated into a particular institute and sharing its particular gift for the life and holiness of the church. Common life includes those structures provided in canon law and the proper law of the institute which enflesh, support, and promote the community life of religious. These structures include a religious house, daily horarium, shared prayer, meals, recreation, and temporalities, and provisions for cloister, dress, and ministry proper to the nature of the institute.

Prior to the Second Vatican Council, common life was stressed both in the universal law for religious and in the constitutions and policies of religious institutes. This emphasis tended to place greater importance on structures and the more juridic aspects of religious life without taking due cognizance of the spirit which these structures and norms were to reflect, support, and help integrate into the lives of the members.

During the ante-preparatory stage of the Second Vatican Council, many bishops made significant observations to the papal secretary of state regarding the rigid structures of women religious in apostolic institutes. Some of the specific items criticized were cumbersome religious habit, horarium out of touch with the apostolate of the religious, too strict cloistral regulations, lack of recreation and rest, poor professional preparation, and inadequate religious formation. The bishops recognized that the 1917 Code of Canon Law had to be revised in order that the norms for religious would allow greater flexibility in women religious institutes of an apostolic nature. These points came to the attention of the bishops throughout the world because they greatly impeded the apostolates of the women religious and precluded their moving into other ministries.[15]

Some religious institutes, refusing to adapt their lifestyles to the teachings of the church and present-day realities, have adhered to a rigid common life, making only minimal changes since the Second Vatican Council. In those institutes where common life has not been evaluated and adapted, religious complain of boredom, stifled human development, a lack of effectiveness in an apostolate antithetical to their lifestyle, and an alienation from clerics, laity, and other religious in the church. Some religious observe that such rigidity, contrary to some beliefs, subtly robs them of the necessary solitude and privacy required for any human being, particularly in an age of tension and stress. Needless to say, these institutes have lost some valuable members who chose to respond to the call of the church to renewal, and the type of candidate entering such institutes today is of serious concern.

There can also be problems if institutes totally abandon the constructs of common life to opt for a more viable community life in their efforts at renewal and adaptation. Rather than attempt the difficult task of adjusting common life to the common good, institutes can simply forsake any semblance of it so that if the members live together, their lifestyle resembles that of an apartment house existence. There is little if any commitment to communal prayer, shared meals, community recreation, and the common use of temporal necessities. If ministries are self-initiated without confirmation from the competent authority of the institute, the vow of obedience and the institute's commitment to a corporate mission are put to serious challenge. The shift from a radical dependence on the structures of common life to a lifestyle free of all the common life supports for the members proves disastrous to the living of religious life. Many of the structures which supported the values of community for religious vanish, and with them the hopes for the ongoing integration of those values in the lives of the members. With such a radical departure from the stability of common life, these religious institutes suffer the departures of their members who want a more stable form of life assured by the very nature of religious life. Likewise, this same lack of stability frequently deters candidates, who may have excellent potential for religious life and want the stability it should afford them, from entering religious life.

Neither of the above descriptions is congruent with the teaching of the church on religious life wherein members live in a Christian community and share life in common. Either of the above extremes will blur and eventually stifle the unique gift of the institute for the life and holiness of the church. Today, there is a great need in society and the church for the witness of true Christian community. By their very nature, religious institutes have a serious responsibility to witness to this fundamental Christian value for the life and holiness of the church.

V. State of Perfection and Christian Development: Profession of the Vows

The potential for human development in the lives of those who make profession of the evangelical counsels is reflected in conciliar teaching:

> At the same time, let all realize that while the profession of the evangelical counsels involves the renunciation of goods that undoubtedly deserve to be highly valued, it does not constitute an obstacle to the true development of the human person but by its nature is supremely beneficial to that development.[16]

The obligation of ongoing formation both on the part of the members and those in authority in religious institutes is stated in the 1983 Code of Canon Law:

Throughout their entire life, religious are to continue carefully their own spiritual, doctrinal, and practical formation, and superiors are to provide them with the resources and time to do this.[17]

The 1917 Code of Canon Law defines the religious state as a stable manner of community life in which the faithful bind themselves to the observance of the evangelical counsels by the vows of obedience, chastity and poverty.[18] Pre-conciliar formation of candidates for the religious life stressed the virtues of the vows: detachment and poverty of spirit; modesty of demeanor and custody of the eyes; the union of one's mind, will and desires with the will of the superior. Seldom was the juridic content of the vow a challenge to be dealt with in the life of the individual religious. Religious, particularly women religious, had little or no personal use of money and other temporal goods apart from what was spent for the common life. Cloistral regulations, the need for a companion on outings, and a corporate apostolate in a hospital, school, orphanage, or social service agency precluded relationships with clerics, laity and other religious. "Blind" obedience, or the unquestioning acceptance of the superior's decision as the will of God, removed the possibility of serious conflicts with those in authority. Religious life, for the most part, was clearly defined with little ambiguity. However, such a lifestyle offered a meager challenge for the Christian development of the members of a religious institute.

A more existential approach to life, the awareness in society and in the church of human dignity, the rights and responsibilities of persons, and developments in the behavioral sciences effected a major shift from a static observance of the vows to an ongoing growth in a life of charity through the practice of the evangelical counsels. Likewise, the rapidity of change, the education of religious, and the specializations in various ministries preclude the former approach to formation in the life of the evangelical counsels. Here again, tension arises with the striving for balance in the lives of religious. Many members of religious institutes have lived for years in a pre-conciliar mode and are making heroic attempts to live a more dynamic life of religious profession. These religious recognize the need for ongoing conversion in their religious commitment. But to initiate radical change without continuity and parameters is to invite disaster into a most delicate lifestyle that requires prayer, study, reflection and constant evaluation.

Admittedly, the experience of religious in the shift from a stable, personal observance of the vowed life to a more dynamic, ecclesial living of the counsels is still in a transitional stage. Present uncertainties evoke strain and tension in individual religious and in religious communities. Likewise, the shift in the living of the vowed life produces misunderstanding and confusion among the faithful and casts doubt on the deliberations of the candidate making a decision for religious life. It should be noted that the candidate for religious life in today's society is very different from the person entering religious life in the pre-conciliar period. This lifestyle now presumes in the potential candidate a certain maturity, with a capacity for ongoing Christian development realized in a deeper conversion to Christ through the practice of the counsels.

Conclusion

Church authorities should be careful to avoid stifling the variety of gifts and the prophetic utterance of religious in the church. Conciliar teaching is most sensitive to this reverence for the gifts of the Spirit, and the revised canon law reflects this reverence in its frequent reference to the proper law of the institute. It is an acknowledged fact that there are a variety of gifts and lifestyles within the major developments of religious life in the church. It seems, too, that more diversity will be accepted within the individual institutes among the members, and the local communities and provinces, as the members strive for greater unity at the most fundamental level of their lives. A rigid uniformity synonymous with a former period of institutionalization in religious life seems no longer appropriate.

The church accepts humbly and gratefully the gift of the evangelical counsels from the Lord, constitutes stable forms of living, and encourages those living the counsels to follow the spirit of their founders. Religious, on their part, must be faithful to their prophetic role in the church. They must represent to the church their unique gifts, as they move beyond accretions, outmoded socio-cultural constructs, and rigid legal formulations. This labor requires prayer, docility to the Spirit in and among the members, cooperation with church authorities, patience, time, and a keen awareness of present-day realities and the needs of God's people.

This struggle is especially critical in women's religious institutes of apostolic life. These institutes are moving away from pre-conciliar structures and norms which never adequately conveyed their gifts and potential to the church. As women take their proper place in society, they cannot be denied it in a church that teaches the fundamental equality of persons and justice in the world. Charisms, the gifts of the Spirit, are carried in fragile earthen vessels. The authorities of the church must trust the generous, searching response of religious to the gifts of God in the midst of transition, confusion, misunderstanding, and misplaced zeal. If the charism is of God, and the efforts at renewal and adaptation are wise and sincere, the gift will surely endure in the hearts of the members, attract others to the religious institutes, and contribute richly to the life and holiness of the church.

Notes

1. *Apostolic Religious Life in a Changing World and Culture,* Fifth Inter-American Conference of Religious. Washington, D.C.: LCWR/CMSM, 1986; Gerald A. Arbuckle, S.M. "Why They Leave: Reflections of a Religious Anthropologist," *Review for Religious* vol. 42, no. 6 (November/December 1983): 815–830; George Aschenbrenner, S.J., "Trends and Issues in a Secularizing World." *Review for Religious* vol. 41, no. 2 (March/April 1982): 186–206; Raymond Hostie, S.J. *The Life and Death of Religious Orders.* Washington, D.C.: CARA 1983; Patricia Willberg, S.C. "Sociology and Religious Life: Call for a New Integration." *Review for Religious* vol. 42, no. 6 (November/December 1983): 846–852.

2. Marie Augusta Neal, S.N.D. *Catholic Sisters in Transition from the 1960's to the 1980's. Consecrated Life Studies 2* (Delaware: Glazier, 1984), pp. 22–23, 76–79; Joseph J. Shields, Ph.D. and Mary Jeanne Verdieck, Ph.D. *Religious Life in the United States: The Experience of Men's Communities.* Washington, D.C.: Cara, 1985: 13, 62–63.

3. *Codex Iuris Canonici Pii X Pontificis Maximi Iussu digestus Benedicte Papae XV auctoritate promulgatus.* Romae: Typis Polyglottis, Vaticanis, 1917 (hereafter cited as 1917 CIC). See cc. 504,4; 506,4; 510; 533,1,1°, 2°; 535,2; 550,2; 552; 607; 643,2; 652,1,3.

4. Austin Flannery, O.P., ed. *Vatican Council II: The Conciliar and Post-Conciliar Documents vols. 1–2.* New York: Costello Pub. Co., 1975, 1982; *Lumen Gentium* 43.

5. *Codex Iuris Canonici auctoritate Ioannis Pauli PP. II promulgatus.* Romae: Liberia Editrice Vaticana, 1983 (here-

after cited as 1983 CIC). See cc. 573,1; 574,1; 575; 576; 577; 590; 607,1,3.

6. 1917 CIC: cc. 487, 488. Note that there is no chapter on the apostolate of institutes in the 1917 CIC comparable to chapter V in book II, part III, section 1, title II of the 1983 CIC.

7. *Mutuae Relationes* 12. See also *Perfectae Caritatis* 1; *Le scelte evangeliche* 5, 21, 24.

8. Pontifical Commission for the Revision of the Code of Canon Law, *Schema of Canons on Institutes of Life Consecrated by Profession of the Evangelical Counsels Draft.* Washington, D.C.: USCC, 1977: XIII–XV.

9. For example, fourteen references are make to the proper law or constitutions of a religious institute in the chapter on government. See cc. 617–630.

10. Francis G. Morrisey, O.M.I. "Introduction," *Religious Institutes, Secular Institutes, Societies of Apostolic Life: A Handbook on Canons 573–746*, edited by Jordan Hite, T.O.R., Sharon Holland, I.H.M., Daniel Ward, O.S.B. Collegeville: The Liturgical Press, 1985, p. 25.

11. *Perfectae Caritatis* 5.

12. c. 677,1.

13. c. 602

14. c. 607,2.

15. *Acta et Documents Concilio Oecumenico Vaticano II Apparando Series I* (*Anterpraeparatoria* vol. 2, pt. 1): pp. 15, 45, 63, 145, 207, 304, 461; vol. 2, pt. 3, p. 102; vol. 3, pt. 4, pp. 90–91.

16. *Lumen Gentium* 46.

17. c. 661.

18. c. 487.

Notes on the Contributors

FATHER CARROLL STUHLMUELLER, C.P. is a member of the Holy Cross Province of the Congregation of the Passion. A well-known writer and lecturer in the field of Old Testament studies, he presently serves on the editorial board of *Bible Today* and on the faculty of the Catholic Theological Union at Chicago.

FATHER JOHN M. STAUDENMAIER, S.J. is an associate professor of the history of technology at the University of Detroit. His *Technology's Storytellers: Reweaving the Human Fabric* (MIT Press, 1985) received the 1986 Alpha Sigma Nu Book of the Year Award for Social Sciences. Father Staudenmaier holds a Ph.D. from the University of Pennsylvania.

ROSE McDERMOTT, S.S.J. is a Sister of St. Joseph, Chestnut Hill, PA, and serves as assistant to the vicar for religious in the archdiocese of Philadelphia. She holds a doctorate in canon law from The Catholic University of America and is a member of the National Conference of Vicars for Religious and the Canon Law Society of America.

MARY ANN DONOVAN, S.C. is a Sister of Charity of Cincinnati and professor of historical theology at the Jesuit School of Theology, Berkeley in the Graduate Theological Union. She is the author of numerous articles, and has a chapter in a forthcoming publication, *Spiritualities of the Heart* (Paulist Press). She is active in the Catholic Theological Society of America and the North American Patristics Society.

MARY EWENS, O.P., a Sinsinawa Dominican, received her master's and doctoral degrees in American studies from the University of Minnesota. For many years she chaired

228

NOTES ON THE CONTRIBUTORS

the American studies department at Rosary College, and subsequently directed Rosary's London Program and its Graduate School of Art in Florence, Italy. Following a term as president of Edgewood College, Milwaukee, Sister Ewens returned to research and teaching as adjunct professor and associate director of the Cushwa Center for the Study of American Catholicism at the University of Notre Dame. She is the author of a number of publications on the American nun, including *The Role of the Nun in Nineteenth-Century America*, and chapters in *Women of Spirit, Women and Religion in America*, Vol. I, *Between God and Caesar, American Catholic Women Then and Now*, and two chapters for North Dakota centennial volumes. She is a former president of the Chicago Chapter, Society of Architectural Historians.

DONALD SENIOR, C.P. is professor of New Testament studies at the Catholic Theological Union in Chicago where he is head of the department of biblical literature and languages and director of the school's Israel study program. He holds a doctorate in New Testament studies from the University of Louvain and has pursued additional study at Harvard University and the Hebrew Union College, Cincinnati. Father Senior is the author of numerous books, including *What Are They Saying About Matthew?* (Paulist Press), is associate editor of *The Bible Today*, book review editor of *The Catholic Biblical Quarterly*, and co-editor of the twenty-two volume international series entitled *New Testament Message*.

JOSEPH H. FICHTER, S.J. is a professor emeritus of sociology at Loyola University, New Orleans. He is one of America's outstanding scholars in both the sociology of religion and the sociology of education. He holds a Ph.D. in sociology from Harvard, has been a Fulbright scholar, held the Chauncy Stillman Chair at Harvard, and was a visiting professor at several universities. Father Fichter is the author of more than twenty books, including *Healing Ministries* (Paulist Press).

SARAH MARIE SHERMAN, R.S.M. is director of life development for her community, the Sisters of Mercy, province of Cincinnati. She served as executive director of the National Sisters Vocation Conference, 1983–1987. She has given numerous workshops and presentations to laity and religious on various aspects of Christian vocation and spirituality.

DIANNE BERGANT, C.S.A. is associate professor of Old Testament at the Catholic Theological Union in Chicago. She is editor of *The Bible Today* and *Collegeville Bible Commentary* (Old Testament series) and author of *Job and Ecclesiastes* (Michael Glazier, 1982), *What Are They Saying About Wisdom Literature?* (Paulist Press, 1984), and *The World Is a Prayerful Place* (Michael Glazier, 1987).

JOHN W. PADBERG, S.J. is director of the Institute of Jesuit Sources in St. Louis. For ten years he was president and professor of church history at Weston School of Theology, Cambridge, MA and he is currently president of the International Conference of Catholic Theological Institutes. Previously he was professor of history and academic vice president at St. Louis University.

REGINA BECHTLE, S.C. is assistant to the president of the Sisters of Charity of New York. Sister Regina, who holds a Ph.D. in theology from Fordham University, has taught theology, spirituality, and women's studies, most recently at Maryknoll School of Theology, Ossining, N.Y. She is a member of the Leadership Conference of Women Religious, the National Assembly of Religious Women, and the Catholic Theological Society of America.

GERALD A. ARBUCKLE, S.M. is professor of cultural anthropology at East Asian Pastoral Institute, Ateneo de

Manila University, Philippines, and involved at present full-time in religious congregational research. Father Arbuckle received his training in cultural anthropology at Cambridge University, and he has had wide research experience in the study of religious congregations and their adjustment problems since Vatican II. His research findings have been published in various reviews, and in his book *Strategies for Growth in Religious Life* (Alba House, 1986).

HOWARD J. GRAY, S.J. is the provincial superior of the Jesuits of the Detroit province and vice president of the Conference of Major Superiors of Men. Prior to his present position, Father Gray served as the rector of the Jesuit community and then dean of the Weston School of Theology, Cambridge, MA. He has lectured and written extensively on religious formation, ministry and pastoral theology.

KRISTIN WOMBACHER, O.P. is prioress general of the Dominican Sisters of San Rafael. She received a doctorate in clinical psychology at St. Louis University. She worked for thirteen years at Napa State Hospital as a clinical psychologist, as well as five years as director of the psychology internship program. Dr. Wombacher does psychological testing, individual and group therapy with religious, and is a psychological consultant to many women's and men's religious congregations. She has given workshops throughout the United States.

JAMES HENNESEY, S.J. is lecturer in religious studies at Canisius College, Buffalo, and rector of the Jesuit community there. Father Hennesey was formerly president of the Jesuit School of Theology in Chicago and professor of the history of Christianity there and at Boston College. He holds a Ph.D. in history from The Catholic University of America. Father Hennesey is the author of several books, including *American Catholics: A History of the Roman Catholic Community in the United States* (Oxford University Press, 1981).

DONNA MARKHAM, O.P. is an Adrian Dominican who is currently serving as a member of the general council for her congregation. She is a licensed clinical psychologist who has spoken nationally and internationally on group psychotherapy and process. Until recently she served as a senior staff psychologist at Sinai Hospital of Detroit. Dr. Markham is the founder and president of the Dominican Consultation Center in Detroit.

LAURIE FELKNOR is managing editor of *Catholic World* magazine, a journal of the Paulist Fathers, in which eleven of these papers first appeared. She has been in religious publishing for the past fourteen years. Ms. Felknor has a degree in English from the University of Missouri and has taught English in high schools and junior college.